PARASOL TREE VILLAGE

JULIA S. LIN

American Literary Press, Inc.
Five Star Special Edition
Baltimore, Maryland

PARASOL TREE VILLAGE

Library of Congress
Cataloging in Publication Data
ISBN 1-56167-569-5

Library of Congress Card Catalog Number:
99-67354

Published by

American Literary Press, Inc.
Five Star Special Edition
8019 Belair Road, Suite 10
Baltimore, Maryland 21236

Manufactured in the United States of America

While passing by,

a man leaves a name;

a swan leaves a song.

THANK-YOU LEAFLETS

Ten thousand thank-you leaflets fall from the parasol tree in Parasol Tree Village along with a deep-deep bow to each of you:

> Joyce Bynum
> Romayne Ponleithner
> Dan Dodobara
> Paul Lorence
> Lisa Lethin
> Jo Anne Busse

Your editing made my Chinese-English tongue more fluent and pleasant throughout the book. Your encouragement worked as a vitamin C— Confidence—for me to continue to write.

> Clyde Higaki
> Gabe Camarillo

You made my peony logo bloom on the pages and the pictures speak words for me.

To

Odosan and Okasan

This book is dedicated to you,
with every passion.

To

Nisan

The clan genealogy, compiled and published
by you, was the resource and inspiration for
writing this book.

To

Charlotte

Enlightened through Reading

An half-acre-sized small pond is open like a clear mirror.

The glorious sky light and the varishaped cloudlets linger in it.

I ask the pond how the water could be so clear.

"There is a source spring that flows life in me."

— Chu Hsi —[1]

---

1. Chu Hsi (1130-1200 A.D.), a great scholar in the Sung Dynasty, is famous for his commentary on the Confucian teachings. My father respected and adhered to them. The poem was translated by the author.

Contents

Prelude

林大伯公派下族譜

祭祀公業 林大伯公鉛

The clan genealogy, the Limb of Lim Dai-pae-kong, opens many interesting chapters through which I may wander, as I ponder and explore.

Prelude

A village, a tiny village, lies in the middle of Taiwan; a village where I have never lived yet love as much as my ancestors did when they were breathing the fresh country air and enjoying the simple and "just-folks" life each sunrise-sunset day.

Today, although their faces have disappeared from the village, I can feel their spirits still living on somewhere, in clouds, in winds, or in trees. These immortal spirits not only guard and guide the villagers but also call forth the ancient virtues: bravery and wisdom. Although their footprints have disappeared long ago into the rice paddies and the thorny paths, I can find traces of them still pressed on the crisscrossed paths in the well-carved rice and crop fields. And these everlasting footprints not only heal and enrich the soil but also usher in and herald the farming seasons: the spring cultivation and the autumn harvest.

On many weekends or holidays, summer or winter breaks, early spring-bloom days, and full autumn-moon nights, my father, a dutiful, henlike widower, used to bring his two youngest chickabiddies, my younger brother Dengjiao and me, to his native hearth—the village. We were either on foot or on his bike for three, picking dew-glistening morning glory or chasing neon-gleaming fireflies, when he came to visit his uncles, aunts, and cousins, or his lifelong teacher, or to attend special family occasions. So I came, I heard, I saw. Gradually, I started to sense, to yearn, to imagine the village life of the past. Today, this yeast-rising yearning extends like a big hand beckoning me back to visit and to explore time and time again. Each time my impression grows more and more.

Although I am linked to the village as by a navel cord and have a passion for exploring the bond, I am merely an espoused daughter. An espoused daughter is like spilled-on-the-ground, uncollectible water,[1] one who has no legitimate position in the paternity-based clan genealogy—switching daughters-in-law with daughters. So I, a *gua-tau-ke-shen-ah*, an outsider, may have no right to talk about my paternal clan-related subjects. However, after picking

---

1. This refers to a custom in Taiwan. On the wedding day, the bride's palanquin (in the old times) or sedan is splashed with a bowl of water when the vehicle is about to leave her maternal home.

up each fallen leaf of the village life-tree and passionately assembling them leaf by leaf once again on its time branches and trunk, the feeling of being an insider grows stronger and stronger. Suddenly, I realize that I am a rich gleaner of information-grain left behind in this small paddy village. Thus, there should be a position for me, an intuitive insider, to share what I have picked up from the ground of my paternal home village.

The clan genealogy, which my eldest brother Deng-piao recently spent years editing and recompiling, opens many interesting chapters through which I may wander, as I ponder and explore. They tell of the passage of the village, the mysterious death of my great-great-great-granduncles, the unsung event and its hero, the 3,133-year-old family line, the legend of the 700-year-old ancient tree, and the spiritual heritage of the Lims. All are honestly and vividly depicted in the clan genealogy. And I, responding to an inner calling, want to share my findings about this village with you.

Now, let me sit on my eyelet-patterned, fine-woven rattan chair, play solo my bamboo flute, and sing this cadenced song "From do-re-mi To la-ti-do":

From a small village to see a big country.

From a family name to reach out to a thousand family names.

From 100^2 years to count back 3,133 years.

From Taiwan to tie to the Tang Mountains.[3]

And so, from the present to meander to the past.

2. The year 1998 is the centennial of my parents.

3. The term "the Tang Mountains" refers to mainland China.

The village name *New-swan-chirr Tseng*, Parasol Tree Village, was derived from the village's two ancient Kgar-dong trees.

.The Lim clan temple in Parasol Tree Village was first built in the early 1800s, and it was rebuilt in 1874.

1. Parasol Tree Village

New-swan-chirr Tseng, literally Parasol Tree Village, was a farm village on the banks of the river Dai-li. It was located in the middle region of Taiwan, between two ferry towns: Leh-tau-diam to the north and Dai-li-khit to the south. And it was a good rest-stop between these two towns at that time when people normally made the journey on foot. By today's measure, it is about seven miles south of Taichung, the fourth largest city of Taiwan and until recently the cultural center of the island.

About 210 years ago, my ancestors came from Fokien, China across the Taiwan Straits and chose to settle in the middle of this yam-shaped, sinuate island. The choice was probably based on the following advantages: the region lay in the center of the island on a big plain with fertile soil, along the ferry river Dai-li, and it was surrounded by lush greenery. Each of these factors played an important role in village life at that time.

Though the river Dai-li was the crucial resource for the paddy field irrigation, it was, unfortunately, also a threatening demon that killed hundreds of lives—both human and animal—when it flooded during the typhoon season. In 1862, the dock of Dai-li was ruined by a flood after a fierce typhoon. Thus, Dai-li-khit declined, and all the trade activities moved from there to a southern town called Ah-dau-bu, which is Bu-hong today.

The village name *New-swan-chirr Tseng* was coined more than two centuries ago. The official "Taiwan Prefecture Records," published in 1741, in the 6th reign year of Cheng-long, recorded that it was the 13th village under the military administration of Fort Ngau-buh, one of ten military forts in Chung-hwa County at that time. So the village was formed sometime during the reign of the emperor Cheng-long,[1] or earlier during his father's time, the emperor Yung-tseng.[2] On September 8, 1950, almost two centuries later, to honor its 700-year-old Kgar-dong tree, the village was renamed *Chirr-ong Tseng*, literally Tree King Village, semantically King Tree Village. But my family has never called it by this new name, although we may

---

1. The reigning title of Emperor Kao-tzong of the Ching Dynasty.
2. The reigning title of Emperor Shi-tzong of the Ching Dynasty.

have used it once or twice as an address the postman to deliver the mail.

People in the old times adopted natural objects or imaginative surroundings to name their villages. The village name *New-swan-chirr Tseng* no doubt was derived from the village's two ancient Kgar-dong trees. The one at the brook-end is today still healthy and thriving, and it is worshipped as a Tree God; the one at the brook-head died two or three generations ago after a severe lightning strike. My eldest brother Deng-piao, as a schoolboy, saw its scorched stump craning out from the brook-bank near a stone bridge. Later, it was totally buried in the ground by new villagers who claimed parts of the river bank as their own farming land. Its gigantic trunk was much thicker and bigger than that of the living one, according to the account of Deng-piao.

The lightning-stricken Kgar-dong tree became the motif of a legend, which was composed by the old villagers to recall its flourishing past and to grieve over its untimely death. And the legend has been passed from mouth to mouth and generation to generation. Today, I wonder how many villagers still know it; therefore, this book has a job to carry it on.

In 1788, in the 53rd reign year of Cheng-long, my great-great-great-grandfather Lim Suii came with his wife Nah Sham and three teenage sons from Fokien, China to Go-dun-leh, after his two younger brothers, Lim Tung and Lim Zuh, had died there in 1784 and 1787, respectively. In 1815, his unmarried third son Lim Tsang, my great-great-grandfather, who was forty at the time, moved from that inauspicious Go-dun-leh to Parasol Tree Village—our blooming village, where he met and married my great-great-grandmother Sun Hah, who was two dozen years his junior. They raised four sons; my great-grandfather Lim Yi-zuh was the third son. After my great-grandmother Liao Twen passed away, Yi-zuh married again. Each of his wives gave him two sons; my grandfather Lim Tsun-zwan was the first son. With my grandmother Tey Tsun, they raised four sons and three daughters, and four daughters from the deceased first wife. (Thank you, clan genealogy! Finally, you mentioned your beautiful daughters.) So, they actually had eleven children; my father Lim Bun-hong was the second son.

In 1933, my father and my mother Lim-Hsiao Pia, who stemmed from a Hollo-Hakka[3] family in a scenic mountain place called Dai-keh about twenty miles north of the village, moved from the village to the city Taichung, with my four elder brothers. My two elder sisters and I and our youngest brother were born later in the city. Having five sons made my father so proud that he thought he had

---

3. The Hollos came from Fokien, and the Hakkas from Quantung.

better luck in male offspring than his forefather who rooted in Taiwan.

Five generations in a total of 145 years lived in this farming village. Today, we joke around and claim that my family were the oldest monkeys in the village, who climbed and swung tree-to-tree through all the village trees.

The first three generations were the citizens of the Ching Dynasty, which spanned the reigns of the six emperors: Cheng-long, Jia-ching, Dau-kwang, Ceng-fong, Tung-tzu, and Kwang-hsu. My grandparents were citizens of both Kwang-hsu of the Ching Dynasty and Mei-zii of the Japanese government. My parents lived under Shiow-kga of the Japanese government and the father-son ruling period of Chiang Kai-shek and Chiang Jin-kou of the Republic of China. They lived forty-seven years as Japanese, and thirty-six years (my father) and five years (my mother who passed away earlier) as Chinese. Why did they become Japanese? And how did my parents turn into Chinese? Who or what drew this fate upon them?

Taiwan had been ruled by Japan for fifty years before it returned to the Republic of China. In 1895, in the 21st reign year of Kwang-hsu, Japan claimed Taiwan as her colony after the Chia-Woo War, or the Sino-Japanese War, in 1894, in which the Ching troops were defeated by the Japanese troops.

Japan had long coveted this pearl-like island on the Pacific Ocean and opened her greedy mouth to swallow it by making grand false accusations. The emperor Kang-hsi had been shortsighted in not seeing this glistening pearl and dreamed of getting rid of it while closing his fat-padded slit eyes at night. He had compared this remote island to itchy scabies—sea pirates and uprisings—attacking a body, which had been stubborn and difficult to clear up.

Now, as a result of the Sino-Japanese War, the emperor Kwang-hsu ruthlessly abandoned his island-people, like dumping a million pairs of worn-out slippers. Too generous, he fed a precious pearl to a ravenous fisher. The formal cession was documented in the Treaty of Ma-kwang in 1895, in which Japan claimed Taiwan and the Pescadores, a small island group called Ma-tzo, named after the Goddess of the Sea, for the so-called reimbursement of the lives lost in the war.

What did my ancestors do for a living? And how was life back then? These and similar questions would ripple in my heart. Because each couple of the first three generations had posthumous titles, we assume they held hereditary honors in official ranks. During the past sovereign times, only the ranked family members could hold titles after they died.

The clan genealogy recorded that the grandmother of Lim Suii was the daughter of the provincial Teh Doh, or Commander-in-Chief. Therefore, his grandfather should either come from a family of equal standing or be an eminent person whose reputation or social status qualified him to marry a Teh Doh's *chien-kgin*, a daughter who is as dear as a thousand pieces of gold. A well-matched family played an important role at that time.

However, in spite of the inherited fortune, life during those primitive, pioneering times was hard and bitter for my ancestors, no matter if they tilled their own soil or hired others to do so. In the clan genealogy the family values, diligence and frugality, were repeatedly emphasized and referred to; hence, we assume that they were living with humble appetites.

Speaking of the family values—diligence and frugality— there is something interesting to mention. These values were faithfully observed by my parents all their life long. And my father drummed these values into us almost every day. Although his drumming stopped in 1984, it is still echoing in our ears. Moreover, each of us has inherited a piece of a 24-karat-gold pendant from him. It is boldly embossed with two characters "Diligence" and "Frugality" on the face and the words "Family Rules" on the back. Now, you know he has made us wear his golden unbreakable rules. Wearing the pendant is not burdensome; observing its implication, frankly enough, is not easy. I try very hard not to enjoy fruit without toil and not to be trapped by the seductive material civilization of this enticing flowering world.

As the eldest son of his parents, my grandfather ran the only grocery store in the village. Although he let the tenants farm on the land he owned, he mastered the art of farming himself. He learned Confucian teachings from the family tutor. He was an intellectual businessman in a farming family.

As the flag of the Rising Sun of Japan flew high in the village, my grandfather's pigtail, a unique Manchu burden of a Ching citizen, was chopped off by order of the new colonizing ruler, the emperor Mei-zii. However, my dear grandpa still dressed in Tang clothing and spoke Taiwanese, or Fokienese—a Chinese dialect and the primary spoken language in Taiwan at the time. Despite his Chinese habits, he was farseeing and not fogyish. He urged his four sons to receive Japanese public school education while calling on the tutor Lim Diau-pin Ceng[4] to teach them Confucian subjects at home. This decision was judicious, especially in a small farming village where many parents kept their children home and gave them only limited education together with an emphasis on manual farming labor.

---

4. Ceng is a respectful form to call a teacher.

My father was born as a Japanese citizen in 1898, in the 31st reign year of Mei-zii. He was a so-called *Nisei*, the second generation, of colonized citizens. He inherited his father's broad-minded character and friendly attitude toward other people. His heart was filled with compassion for the people who had less luck. Many times I saw him chatting with a beggar who came to ask for a bowl of food, while the beggar was eating his bowl of fresh food. He worked for a short time in his teen years as an interpreter in the office of the Taiwan governor-general and then served for about thirty years as an expert in rice-related subjects in the government offices during the Japanese ruling time.

In 1945, after World War II, Taiwan was returned to China. My father was happy about becoming the citizen of his own fatherland, but he soon found himself just a forty-seven-year-old ex-Japanese public official and a non-Mandarin-speaking inferior citizen. The language, the thousand-year-old Hollo[5] language, which had been a state language used in the Tang Dynasty, was not accepted by the new, Mandarin-speaking government. The Mandarin-speaking mainlanders, who followed President Chiang Kai-shek to Taiwan when the mainland was taken over by Mao Tse-tung in 1949, occupied the higher public posts. Since the social system changed dramatically, instead of serving in a public post, my father accepted a position as an

---

5. The word "Hollo" is created by the author to refer to the place, the people, and the culture that originated 5,000 years ago in the basin between the Yellow River and the River Lo. It is known also as the Central Plains. Hol = River = Yellow River; Lo = River Lo, a tributary of the Yellow River.

executive administrator in managing property for a well-known Lim family (not related), where he loyally worked for fifteen years until this Lim family moved its enterprise from Taiwan to Japan. My father retired at the same time.

Although the village was only a small farming village, it produced several well-read young men. The boys of the village learned traditional Sinology from their fathers or family tutors. They studied for years and eagerly hoped that one day they could pass the imperial examination and be given honorary ranks to serve in the imperial court.

In the reign of Kwang-hsu, my great-great-uncle Lim Quan-hu'ng was elected as one of the top marshals by passing the imperial examination in Beijing. The election was regarded as a big honor at that time, especially because he came from a remote village beyond the sea. However, it was an irony of fate that the newly elected imperial marshal himself died of poor health. Before beginning to serve in the post, he perished like a flaming star, gleaming visible for a short moment and falling with a long, long sigh.

Later, my youngest great-uncle, Lim Keng-sheng, was another poor soul, whose fate was controlled by unfavorable destiny. He dedicated his young life to prepare for the imperial examination, but his ambition was doused when the emperor Kwang-hsu presented Taiwan to Japan. Overnight, my great-uncle became an illiterate Japanese by force. This well-learned scholar, whose mind was spun and woven with Confucian subjects, lived a melancholy life and died in his seventies.

There were only two family names in the village during my grandparents' time: the Lims (the Woods), and the Chous (the Stones); ninety percent of the villagers were Lims. They fenced themselves in with two ringlike bamboo groves, which were known in the nearby area as the "Big Bamboo Rings." The villagers knew each other very well since they were all related to each other. The houses were built mostly using hay or reeds for roofing—rust tiles were used later during my parents' time—and the unburnt clay-hay bricks for the walls—treated bricks were adopted later as the material became popular. The houses were settled along the bank of the village brook, which murmured as it gently flowed into the main river Dai-li.

Cultivated in the village fields for generations were the basic crops: rice, sugar cane, and sweet potatoes and the alternate crops: corn, casaba, peanuts, and tobacco. A variety of vegetables and fruits were cultivated in the garden of each house. Every family raised its own cows, pigs, chickens, ducks, geese, and turkeys. The village brook supplied abundant anchovy, carp, catfish, clam, eel, shrimp, *ke-koh*, *ko-kam*, red-eye *chiu*, and even frogs were found under the weed-covered brook banks or in the paddy fields.

Fishing in the brook was a favorite after-school pastime. Not only did it bring great joy to my eldest brother and my cousin Deng-chiu, but the boys' catches were transformed by my mother into many delectable and nutritious dishes for the dinner table.

When speaking of my mother, my compressed data, collected by the accounts of my sisters Shiu-kim and Shiu-bue, instantly expand their scenes. Although half a century has passed, to repeat each scene of my mother's life I still have pain in my inmost heart: eating the leftover meals and saving fresh ones for us during that food shortage wartime, preparing breakfast at 4:00 A.M. for my second brother Deng-tzun,[6] who worked for a while out of the city, lifting up a cumbersome bamboo steamer, pedaling steadily on the Singer sewing machine, splitting the stove firewood, carrying buckets of water for the vegetable garden, trimming branches from the fruits and flowering trees. She was a delicate and soft-hearted woman who did many physical harsh chores to provide for her family and gave us a spiritual shelter, warm and fragrant, during her short lifetime. She also would lend her hands to help neighbors, as they have told me many times.

---

6. To stop my mother from getting up early, he had to harden his heart and refused to eat. Then, my dear mother was in tears over her son left house for work with an empty stomach.

Other than the aged Kgar-dong trees, the fish-teeming, resourceful brook, and the scholarly farmers, the village had a private Lim clan temple and a common cemetery; both are still in place today.

The Lim clan temple was sponsored and dedicated by the ancestress Nan Kuan-neun, the daughter of the provincial Commander-in-Chief, to her fiancé. For some unknown reason, her fiancé Lim Guan-teh, the first son of the family, died suddenly, so it was arranged for her to marry the second son, Lim Guan-jiang. There were actually two reasons for her to build the temple. First, it was to dedicate it to her lost fiancé. She did not want his lonely soul wandering around with no roof to shelter him, becoming a hungry ghost if no one worshipped him with food. Second, it was for her two beloved grandsons, Lim Tung and Lim Zuh, who died unmarried in Taiwan before she did. She and her husband raised seven sons; she lived 110 years, 1667-1777, but her husband lived only 62 years, 1667-1729.

Lim Tien-tzung was their first son and the father of Lim Suii. The family tree then branched off and was referred to as the Limb of Lim Dai-pae-kong. Dai-pae-kong was actually the posthumous title of her fiancé; literally, "Dai" means great, "pae" is a noble title like a count, and "kong" is a respectful form to deify a deceased male. The Limb of Lim Dai-pae-kong comprised the seven branches of their sons; a generation later, it became only six branches since the sixth son had no descendants.

In fulfilling their grandmother's will, the offspring of her six sons used part of her private savings to build the clan temple after they settled down in Parasol Tree Village. They also used her savings to purchase three *jia* (one *jia* is about one hectare) of good farmland. The income from this farmland was used to maintain the temple and the temple-related activities. What foresight she had!

The clan temple was first built in the early 1800s with a plain hay roof and was named "the Lim Restoration Common Hall." It was rebuilt in 1874 with a colorful tile roof, legendary figurines, and cloud-kissing dragons and treetop-flying phoenixes above the splendid façade. It was renamed "the Successive Restoration Hall." Because of leaks on rainy days and cavities bored by hungry termites, this almost 200-year-old clan temple will soon be rebuilt with modern facilities, designed by my third brother Deng-kinm, a famed and recently retired architect in Taichung, to ease the work of maintenance. I find it a pity to demolish this classic building.

The common cemetery was located outside the village. All my ancestors rest there after their hard pioneering life in the new world of Taiwan to fulfill their dreams of a better life. Again, I am told that all my ancestors' bones will soon be collected and buried in a private graveyard.

The neighboring town Dai-li-khit had a common cemetery, too. It is said that this yard was once the residence of Lim Sung-bun, a leader of an uprising against the Cheng-long regime. He was executed in 1787 in Beijing, and his residence was later razed to the ground.

Nothing is constant; all things vary constantly with time and external conditions. Although the village brook still murmurs into the river Dai-li, the faces and the hearts of the village have totally changed.

In the past forty years, the village has gradually evolved from a rural farm village to a light industrial suburban town. Today, one hears not roosters crowing at dawn but cars honking, not water-cows bellowing in paddy fields but tractors rumbling; one smells not fresh rice hay mingled with cow manure but chemical odors; one sees not a clear blue sky with floating cloudlets but a gloomy sky tainted by smog. The villagers today can hardly imagine that here was once an idyllic farm village, pleasantly picturesque in natural simplicity and stillness. Yet this rustic, idyllic picture will always live in the memory of each member of my family.

The emperor Cheng-long (1711-1799), the fourth emperor of the Ching Dynasty of China, became emperor in 1735. He reigned until 1796, a total of sixty years.

(This picture is scanned from The Smithsonian Catalogue)

2. The Emperor and the Parasol Trees

The emperor Cheng-long (1711-1799), the fourth emperor of the Ching Dynasty of China, became emperor in 1735. He reigned until 1796, a total of sixty years. He abdicated out of respect for his grandfather, the emperor Kang-hsi, who had ruled the dynasty for sixty-one years. However, the emperor Cheng-long still held power behind the scenes until his death in 1799. Under the first decade of his rule the leaves were greener and more prosperous, but then the dynasty gradually declined because he was troubled with foolish, sun-reaching ambition—leading ten battles for territorial expansion, including one to crack the rebellion in Taiwan. To expand his territory into Central Asia, he became a warmonger, squandering both innocent lives and national funds.

He was born as Hong-li, the fourth son of his father, the emperor Yung-tseng, and one among about a hundred grandsons of his grandfather. Hong-li was a good-looking, refined, and bright young boy. At age twelve, he first met his grandfather in Yuan-Ming-Yeng, the Summer Palace. The grandfather liked him at first sight and let him live in his own palace, where he himself instilled everything in young Hong-li's bright mind and appointed him to be the successor to the throne after his father.

He liked travel and was a discriminating gourmet. He was a good horseman and a skilled archer. He wielded both pen—writing prose and poetry—and sword—leading troops into battle. His great library collection numbered 36,000 volumes. His nine trips, traveling incognito to Chiang-nan, the entire area south of the Yangtze River, for sightseeing and better understanding of his remote land and subjects, are meticulously documented by the historians. Stories of the trips, true or false, have been repeatedly narrated by bourgeois storytellers at tea-houses, and they have been scripted and filmed many times by film producers.

There are many anecdotes about his life that are probably fictitious but nonetheless fascinating. They include a romance with a sensible wine-house girl; Robin-Hood-like adventures of helping the poor and fighting for justice; the plain dishes of a peasant kitchen, which he ate with great relish; and a gesture by the eunuchs, disguised as common people, of nodding two crooked fingers, representing two kneeling feet, on tables in tea-houses after having been served by the emperor, disguised also as a common person. Today this gesture is commonly used by guests in restaurants to show appreciation for waiters' or companions' service.

Two versions of the legend about the emperors and the Kgar-dong trees, or the Parasol trees, have emerged over time in the village. The vivid, authentic version, describing the emperor Cheng-long's journey to Parasol Tree Village, lives in my family's heart. The dull, newer version, depicting the unpleasant journey of the emperor Jia-ching, son of the emperor Cheng-long, is engraved on an ebony stone erected beside the Kgar-dong tree. My family favors the authentic version, since it leaves one with a bittersweet and helpless feeling, sighing for that once flourishing and then doomed Kgar-dong tree.

We assume neither of these two emperors actually traveled across the Taiwan Straits, nor did they come all the way from the golden Forbidden City, Beijing, to visit this remote and desolate frontier village. So, we believe that to season the simple and plain village life, the ancient village storymaker elaborately built up a make-believe story for self-amusement and also to entertain the others. But you never know—for an active boy like Prince Hong-li, some impossible things could have actually happened. Thus, the famous nine trips to Chiang-nan may have been actually ten trips, with a secret trip to overseas Taiwan. Who knows?

Let's start with the first legend, which talks about the emperor Jia-ching's adventure in the village.

The emperor Jia-ching (1759-1820) was on his way to an unknown destination. As he and his men came close to Parasol Tree Village, he was suddenly attacked by bandits. A mysterious fellow, clad in red with his face veiled, who was standing at the top of the Kgar-dong tree, shouted loudly at the bandits and swooped down upon them. He shooed them away, and the emperor's life was saved. The emperor rose up from the ground to express thanks from his heart, but he couldn't find this red-cloaked fellow. It seemed that he had disappeared into nowhere. None of his company could say where he went. They looked for him in the nearby area but failed to find even a footstep. Therefore, the emperor believed that this brave, husky, red-clad fellow must have been a transformation of the tree itself. For this reason, the emperor conferred upon this tree the title of "Tree King."

*　　*　　*　　*　　*

The following legend, about the emperor Cheng-long's journey to the village, is the one told at the dinner table of many family get-togethers by my father's father, then by my father, and now by my brothers to their children.

On a fiery summer day, Prince Hong-li, sitting in a plain bamboo palanquin, and his squad, marching in file in a cloud of dust, were on their way to the ferry-town Dai-li-khit. They walked through acres of man-tall, cotton-white flowering reeds, nodding drowsily in the heat waves, passed miles of waist-high, pomegranate-red thornberries, slouching listlessly in the glinting rays, and trod on a carpeting of sensitive, prickly mimosas. The weary and exhausted squad found no shelter from the cloudless high-sun-sky in the never-never-outskirts of the village.

Finally, they saw a gigantic tree as they approached the village. When they reached the tree, they found that there was not only a grand old tree, but also a crystal-clear, meandering freshwater brook flowing gently under it. Hundreds of buoyant, large-headed, and scaleless catfish were swimming in the brook with their whisker-like barbels, swelling gills, and wiggling tails. The weary and sweating men shouted exultantly and plunged into the fish-crowded cool brook, splashing playfully in it. The large-headed and scaleless catfish, agitated by this sudden commotion, swam swiftly and agilely away. As the splashes ceased, some of the fish peeked, some peeped, and some peered from under the water weeds.

Suddenly, the canopy-like grand old tree, oddly enough, eclipsed the high sun. Its boughs and twigs were dancing in the air full of glee, and its leaves were rustling in the gentle breeze all around—shur. . . shur. . . shur. . . . Prince Hong-li was so pleased with this pleasant coolness and gentle breeze that he thought it was a blessing from the grand old tree. He wiped the sweat from his forehead and face with a yellow silk handkerchief, lying with his back against the grand old tree. His eunuchs and the squad sat around the grand old tree. In their wet and loose clothing, they stretched themselves out to relieve and to recharge their overrun legs. Shur. . . shur. . . shur. . . ; quickly, the weary, drowsy men were lulled into sleep by this opium-like melody.

As Prince Hong-li awoke, he felt totally recovered from the exhausting half-day journey; he felt refreshed and vital once again. He limbered himself up and glimpsed instinctively skyward; immediately he yelled loudly: "Isn't it a parasol tree?" He jumped up, walked around the grand old tree, and began to study its strong body-trunk, its arching limb-boughs, its dense vein-twigs, and its glossy knuckle-leaves. Then he praised the grand old tree with a passionate voice: "What a magnificent tree! What a Tree King!" He was deeply impressed by this high-spirited grand old tree.

In thanks for the blessing of coolness from the grand old tree, the prince promised to confer a title if he one day were crowned emperor. Before the procession set off, he bowed three times and murmured his promise to the grand old tree. Then the prince ordered his eunuchs to honor the grand old tree with a big, red sash around its shoulder-boughs. Now, the grand old tree stood stately with a perky look—its twigs were swinging animatedly in the air, and its leaves were glossier and silkier than ever.

Several summers passed, and Prince Hong-li was crowned with great pomp as Emperor Kao-Tzung of the great Ching of China, with his reigning title as Cheng-long. He became a highly popular sovereign and ruled his great land in prosperity (at least some describe it so) for sixty years officially, and three more years after abdication as a puppet master—the longest rule of all times. The memory of the hot, sticky trip to Taiwan and the coolness from the grand old tree clung firmly to his heart. The promise of conferring a title hovered in his mind for years. And now it was time to fulfill it.

One flaming midsummer day, the young emperor sent his messengers to Taiwan to carry out his promise. Unfortunately, the messengers could not remember the exact location of the grand old tree. They came from the opposite direction by water and were fooled and misled by the visual appearance of a parasol-like giant tree that stood by the brook-end. Instantly, they thought that this giant tree must be the one honored with a red sash by the emperor Cheng-long, who had been Prince Hong-li. So the chief messenger and his fellow messengers conferred a title upon it with no second thought.

The ceremony was held with several aged villagers as honorary delegates and dozens of common villagers as spectators. They started by burning three long sticks of incense and three bows for gratitude, then offered fragrant flowers for vitality, fresh fruits for purity, and peach-shaped rice cakes for longevity. After three long sticks of incense had burned, the chief messenger unrolled the firman and proclaimed: "With this decree to acknowledge you on your merits for giving *Zhen*[1] a great favor, when *Zhen* was in an out-of-control circumstance caused by mother nature. *Zhen*, the Emperor of the Great Ching, confer upon you the title 'Tree King.' And *Zhen* do firmly want to name this village after your unique characteristics. So, *Zhen* name it 'Parasol Tree Village.'" This sonorous, quick-tongued proclamation, barking up the wrong tree, ended with a peal of roaring claps, which were as loud as summer thunder.

Because the proclamation came from the emperor's golden, godlike mouth, this lucky giant tree has continued to thrive and flourish in the village until today.

Just two miles away at the brook-head, the heartbroken grand old tree watched the whole ceremonious session

---

1. *Zhen* means I (subjective) or me (objective) and was used only by an emperor.

with a sullen face. He was very sad and frustrated, heaving helpless sighs. But there was nothing he could do except perhaps to cast a voodoo-hoodoo magic spell in huffing, puffing, and blowing them away. No, no, no, he wouldn't do that for he was a noble tree. So he would do no harmful thing to a life, even an ant.

As the lofty summer lotus faded away on the red-hot day and the sad cicada cried shrilly in the dark muggy night, the once green, glossy, and singing leaves became rusty, dull, and mute. As the sweet autumn osmanthus were fanned out by the monsoon and the legendary hare pounded the immortal herb monotonously and lonesomely in the pale moon, the rusty, dull, and mute leaves fell leaf by leaf, one after another; the once strong and solid trunk turned shaky and hollow because its *chi*, its vitality, had evaporated from its core, which was inflamed with melancholic self-pity. As the hardy winter plums suffered from the biting frost, and the white petals dispersed around the earth like dead silk cocoons, this hapless grand old tree quietly ascended higher, higher, and higher above the village. As the opulent spring peonies bloomed in full on a clear cloudless day, a handsome butterfly[2] was seen dancing hither and thither around the fragrant flowers.

*   *   *   *   *

2. The author makes this handsome butterfly out to be the transformation of the grand old tree, adopting the work of Chuang-tzu (369 - 295 B. C.), the Taoist philosopher, who preached Taoism after Lao-tzu (604 - 531 B.C.), a renowned philosopher and founder of Taoism.

It is a shame that this original version is unknown today. But it is my hope that the legend will be mouth-spread, paper-written, cartoon-filmed, and even stone-engraved; furthermore, I hope that a shining ebony stone tablet inscribing this story can be displayed openly next to the existing one in a row, side by side.

In the village this ancient Kgar-dong tree is respectfully called *Chirr Ong Kong,* or Tree King God. He has been revered and worshipped as a Tree God for many generations.

3. The Tree King God

The name "Parasol Tree Village" is derived from a 700-year-old Kgar-dong tree, a deciduous tree with heart-shaped, shiny jade-green leaves and clusters of white, pealike flowers. "Kgar-dong" is locally used in Taiwan to refer to the tree. The tree name is written as 槐 in Chinese, (木 = tree, 鬼 = ghost) and pronounced as "Hwai." So, it is a ghost tree, referring to its spooky, towering shape, which strongly resembles both a ghost and a pagoda. Thus, it is also known as a Chinese Pagoda tree. Its Latin name is Bischoffia Javanica, according to the tablet that is displayed by the tree.

The Hwai tree has a very long life. In mainland China today, you can find some of them as old as a thousand years or more. The ancient Chinese scholars liked it very much and named it the "Scholar Tree." They even named the fourth month of the year the *Hwai-yueh*, Hwai-moon. Its gallant and stately appearence has been admired by many masculine hearts since ancient times. There was an emperor of the Hsia Dynasty in 2040 B.C. who named himself "Emperor Hwai." The first three dynasties, Hsia, Shang, and Chou originated in the area called "Hollo" located in the Yellow River delta by its two tributaries: the Lo and the Yee rivers. Because of this far-reaching history, people assume the Hwai tree must be native to the Hollo region and call it the "Hollo Tree," and they say, "Where the Hans are, there are Hwai trees."

The Kgar-dong tree in Parasol Tree Village measures 7 meters 10 centimeters in circumference, about an embrace of seven outstretched school-boy-arms, and 15 meters in height. Amazingly, seven different symbiotic plants grow on it, which brings a colorful, gorgeous array when their flowers bloom in spring and summer. It is really a feast for the eyes and the mind. But this spectacular scene is now on the wane since the tree has lost several limbs to lightning. Yet it still stands stately by the brook-end and has been documented as one of the two most ancient trees in the Taichung Basin.

In the village this ancient Kgar-dong tree is respectfully called *Chirr Ong Kong*, or Tree King God. He has been revered and worshipped as a Tree God for many generations. And the villagers do not regard him as decayed and senile; in fact, they believe he is still green and vigorous. He has daily chores to do and is quite a busy old man.

Every so often, the villagers come to the Tree King God to request favors. The favors are on a variety of sticky subjects, including keeping family members in good health, promoting happiness, guarding rice paddies for a larger harvest, continuing the family line (asking for a son), choosing a suitable son-in-law who has a magic wand to wave to turn a black raven into a rainbow phoenix or a meager daisy into a grand peony, picking the right daughter-in-law who has a wonder incubator (womb) to hatch either a crawling snake (mediocrity) egg into a flying dragon (prodigy) or a clay-tile (girl) fetus into a jadeite (boy), rescuing someone from a failing business, helping school children to pass the entrance examination, making a decision whether a trip should be taken, finding the rustler who stole the plow cow days ago, or even providing the right way out of a dilemma.

I am the Tree God's believer, too; I don't think he is decayed and senile with no spirit. You see, I have prayed to him to blow away each peony-scented leaf of this book worldwide. And now he has fulfilled my wish—people like you, ten thousand miles away, have smelled these leaves and are reading these lines. So, I am right; he has spirit. And I have to light incense again; yes, yes, yes, I have to bow to him and thank him deeply.

To communicate with the Tree God, the worshippers light incense and murmur their requests. Then they toss a pair of *Sing-pwei*, divining blocks, on the ground to read the prophesied oracle of the Tree God. The *Sing-pwei* are a pair of wooden or bamboo blocks in a crescent shape. The blocks are normally lacquered with the inner flat part, Yin, in red and the outer curved part, Yang, in black. The Yin-Yang is a body of the dual parts that represents the two opposing principles in nature: feminine-masculine, moon-sun, night-day, shade-light, north side of a mountain-north side of a stream, the underworld-the earthly world. The Yin is negative and the Yang is positive; only the balanced dual parts, fifty-fifty, can create a harmonious whole.

To toss the *Sing-pwei* blocks, you hold the two flat parts face-to-face and after you have spoken your request and bowed to the Tree God, toss them on the ground to read the oracles: two red-flat-sides up is a laughing *pwei*, which means the request is not yet processed, or the Tree God is busy at the moment, so you must light incense again and try again later; two black-curved-sides up is an angry *pwei*, which means the Tree God does not agree with the request, so don't take action; one red-flat-side up and one black-curved-side up is a matched *pwei*, which means the Tree God does agree with the request, so go ahead and do it.

For many generations, the villagers practiced a ritual upon the birth of a baby boy. It is said that today this custom is still observed by the villagers, but I doubt if it is done in the same way as it was by the villagers of old.

All the village boys were guarded under the blessing of the Tree King God. On the Mid-Autumn Festival, the 15th day of the 8th moon of the lunar calendar, the parents of the newborn baby boys received an amulet from the Tree King God Club. The amulet is an antique finished metal pendant in a shape of a leaf of the parasol tree with three embossed bold characters "Tree King Medal" against a textured or floral-veined background and strung with red yarn lace. Then, the villagers went to *pai-pai*, light incense to god, and begged the Tree God to guard the newborn baby boy. The parents of the older boys went to *pai-pai* and thanked the Tree God for having been well-guarded during the past year and begged for continuation of their good fortune.

The *pai-pai* course for guarding the village boys was accomplished with majestic rituality. (It was really an example of sex discrimination: a boy was as precious as a jadeite, and a girl was as worthless as a clay-tile.) According to the recollection of my brother Deng-piao, it was performed with the steps shown below:

1. First, all the offerings were placed on the table, followed by offering three tiny cups of jasmine tea or rice wine, lighting two red pencil-tall candles, and giving the Tree God three deep bows while holding three incense sticks, which brought a smell of sandalwood.

The offerings included: a box of moon cakes, a pastry specially baked for that very day—the Mid-Autumn Festival; a plate of freshly picked fruits from the house yard; a small dish of sweet osmanthus, *Guey-hwa*, the flower of the eighth moon and for which the month is named *Guey-yueh*; and several stacks of gold-stamped and silver-stamped spirit money, paper money to be burnt for the deceased or gods.

2. When the incense burned down half-way, the parents replaced the old red yarn lace with new lace and burned the new lace at both ends until there were burn-marks, which means the amulet has been registered. Next, they begged the Tree God for a couple of leaves and attached them to the amulet. Finally, they hung it around the boy's neck to activate its good luck charm.

   The red yarn lace was renewed on a yearly basis until the boy reached maturity at sixteen. Deng-piao still keeps his amulet, and it is the 79th anniversary (80th, with Chinese counting) on the Mid-Autumn Festival this year, 1999.

3. As the incense burned, the worshippers tossed the divining blocks until a matched *pwei* was displayed. Then, they burned the gold-silver spirit money on the ground and later spilled three drops of jasmine tea or rice wine over the ashes of the spirit money. The ritual ended with the joyous lighting of deafening firecrackers.

Most of the time, you see the ashes of the gold-silver money whirling and dancing in the air with the autumn wind, and then disappearing into nowhere. Of course, the Tree God knows where they go.

The burning of spirit money to worship gods or the deceased is a popular custom which has been practiced for several hundreds of years. Usually, spirit money is burned sheet-by-sheet from a stack of 50 or 100, but on some special occasions piles or tons have been burned. Some people even, time-consumingly, roll it sheet-by-sheet in the form of gold or silver bars.

Recently, a radical said that this custom is wasteful of both time and real money. He suggested "Why not let the spirits cash money from either a Visa or a MasterCard?" He explained "With this handy way one needs only to burn two cards to one's beloved god or ancestors, who, in turn, can then cash the money with any amount they need."

The "Tree King God Club" was really the "Lim Club," a proprietary club. It was managed by a panel of six delegates, each of whom represented his own branch family of the six branches of Lim Dai-pae-kong. The delegates of the panel were reelected yearly by voting or taking turns. The panel was responsible for coordinating and managing the Lim activities. The club budget came from the harvest sale of rice, twice a year, and the other crops, year-round, which were raised on the previously mentioned 3-*jia* farmland owned by the clan temple. Thus, the cost of the club activities was financed and supported by the club itself.

The club meeting was held in the Lim clan temple on the same day as the renewing of the red yarn lace of the amulet, the Mid-Autum Festival. It functioned as a day for everybody to look back and to think of their ancestors; it was also a day for everybody to get rid of the stress caused by hard work and to become relaxed; furthermore, it worked as a day for everybody to get together in a reunion.

On a yearly basis, each family took a turn hosting a luncheon party. The dishes, usually ten or twelve, were not served on tables but were placed on the ground on large, round bamboo trays that were about three foot in diameter. The meal-takers were not allowed to sit on chairs; every one squatted while eating the meal. About ten people, young and old, squatted around a tray, and a typical luncheon featured ten such trays.

The purpose of serving the meal on the ground was to let everyone relive firsthand the bitter life that their ancestors had experienced in pioneer days. It was also to let each one comprehend the essence of the old proverb: "Sweet fruit comes after bitter root." "Happy sunny days come after sweating away." "Drink water, think of its origin." "No pain, no gain. "

In addition to the luncheon party, the club had other duties. It sponsored both the Spring and the Autumn Sacrifice Rites, helped members who encountered a sudden mishap, and created work opportunities by employing its members to work in the farm fields owned by the clan temple.

The club ceased to exist many years ago. We can't remember exactly when and how, but we have concluded that these factors played a part: The majority of the Lims moved from the village to the big cities. The social system changed from the simple, slow-paced farming life to complex, fast-paced, trade-industrial life. The new generation found that "squatting and eating ground food" was not very enjoyable. My eldest brother feels ashamed because he has not been able to keep the club alive for this generation. But at least at the yearly Spring and Autumn Sacrificial Rites, the Lims can still get together twice a year in the village.

Because the Kgar-dong tree has such historic value, the county office Dai-li has been asked to protect him with modern facilities. A lightning rod has been installed on his head, a small cement wall has been wrapped around his body, and the ground has been paved to cover his feet, his roots. Now that the tree wears an armor of steel and stone, lightning and thunder have to make a detour around him. And those *love-it-to-death* fanatics have no way to hurt his body or feet while burning incense or spirit money for him. Their earlier burning scars are still visible.

Recently, a recreational pavilion has been built, which serves as an amusement park for the visitors who come to admire this rare and unique ancient tree. The original tiny shrine by his side has been transformed into a small modern temple at his back.

From a natural and spiritual point of view, the Kgar-dong tree used to be a sight for soothing sore eyes and a shrine for inspiring visitors with its life and its strength. But with all these modern facilities, the picture has been ruined and the inspiration has been stifled.

The Kgar-dong tree has been standing quietly in the village for about seven hundred baking summers and chilling winters. He has seen hundreds of villagers come and go. He has listened to winds laugh and rains cry from all four directions. He has smelled stinky manure in the past and chemical odors today. He has shared the happiness and the sorrow of the villagers. He is a real Tree God and does himself proud: aged but still vigorous, deformed but yet green. He is the guardian of the village. And he embodies the village's spiritual and physical heritage now and forever.

Carp, silver or gold, motifs are often found on paintings, jade carvings, in poems and as ornaments in garden. It is believed to be an auspicious creature who brings fortune and luck. This painting is created by my sister Shiu-kim to wish a Happy New Year.

4. Grow a Foot a Night

My grandmother was a masculine woman, but that does not mean she was a successful career-oriented woman or a radical head-in-the-clouds feminist who led an extreme women's liberation movement. On the contrary, she was a typical old-fashioned Chinese woman who was responsible for the greasy work in the kitchen, and who shouldered the tedious daily household chores. Actually, she was the kitchen manager who led a team of three daughters-in-law in preparing and cooking three daily meals on a troublesome, wood-burning clay stove. Under her management, the three daughters-in-law got along with each other and cooperated very well. Therefore, the three daily meals were cooked with love and laughter. My grandmother was also the recreation manager who planned and arranged the festive occasions and lifeways of a family of some twenty members. Yet she was capable of keeping her inherent femininity in social conversations with men, unique in that very reserved, conservative time and man-dominated world. Her combined feminine-masculine character was surprisingly admired and respected by the villagers, young and old.

She came from a Hakka family and was the second wife of my grandfather, who married her after his first wife died and left him with four young daughters. From her picture one can tell she had a pretty face with a Western look. She was very strict about the children's behavior, whether at home or at outside occasions. Her philosophy for bringing up children was "Nature needs nurture," which means the original good nature a child possesses could be changed into a mean or even evil disposition if it lacked proper nurture. For example, she said a child is like a tender vine that you can easily bend to form the way or shape you want it to grow on an arbor; otherwise, once it grows older and stronger, it will be intractable.

Although none of the women in the village at that time received a formal education, my grandmother made herself the master of nursery rhymes, which were not only enjoyed by her own children but were also passed on to us through my parents and my third aunt, who was in her early seventies and who came often to visit us for a month at a time. My father had great love and respect for his sister, who was at least ten years older than he, even though they did not have the same mother.

Nursery rhymes can open and fill in a small child's blank heart and can also sweeten and brighten a young life. They can be a very positive influence on a small, developing mind with boundless, creative imagination. Some nursery rhymes burst with life and humor through personified animals, plants, planets, or natural phenomena, such as wind, cloud, lightning, thunder, snow, and rain; some of them narrate a story, an adventure, a description of a special occasion, or just merely a piece of a dream. Most of them are recited with rhyme; some of them have little meaning, but merely an emphasis on the rhyme.

It is regrettable to say that the nursery rhymes that have been recited in past generations are being forgotten in Taiwan today. Although some of them can be found or retrieved through the long-faint memory of older people, they are mostly incomplete or not original. The decline is the effect of changing government systems, first the Japanese-speaking government and then later the Mandarin-speaking government. For about one hundred years Taiwanese was officially forbidden in schools. The school children during these two government stages found it uncomfortable to learn, recite, or sing the Taiwanese nursery rhymes and thought they were too rustic and old-fashioned.

Today, just because they are rustic with a beauty in simplicity, I find they are worth resurrecting to ease this hectic, rhymeless electronic life. They are actually the lost spiritual and cultural treasures of the past. They have enriched my childhood and have been beneficial to my life in many ways. So I am sure they would be beneficial to others, too.

Let me translate two nursery rhymes that both are about the carp. The carp, silver carp or gold carp, is a favorite motif in Chinese gardens, paintings, and nursery rhymes. The first one is recited in Hollo and the second one is recited in Kakka. Although there is no rhyme in the English translation, from the verse you can tell it is fun and enjoyable to recite.

The Wedding of a Carp

It is gloomy;
it is going to rain.

A carp wants to marry a wife.

The sand turtles hold lamp-poles;
The water turtles beat drums.
The dragonflies hold up rainbow flags;
The mosquitoes blast pipes.
The frogs carry the palanquin on their shoulders
with two eyes popping up;
Each of them eats a rice-dumpling and cries out for help.

The palanquin is carried into the hall.
The groom bows to the elder brother;

The elder brother does not wear a skirt.
He bows to the dragon boat;
The dragon boat is "poo-poo" flying.
He bows to the teakettle;
The teakettle is "chiang-chiang" boiling.

There is a girl behind the door
who quietly makes up her face.

In the Brilliant Moonlight

In the brilliant moonlight,
A shiu-tzai-long[1] rides on a white horse
and passes a lotus pond.
Behind the lotus pond are planted a lot of leeks.
The leek flowers are tied and sent to the in-law house.
In front of the in-law house is a fish pond.
Many of the carp in the fish pond are eight feet long.
The longer ones are caught to pan-fry and eat with wine.
The shorter ones are caught to present to the bride.

By the account of my third aunt, the people in the Parasol
Tree Village had a great passion for reciting nursery
rhymes, inspired by my grandmother. On summer nights

---

1. It was an official rank of a talented and virtuous man who passed the
former civil service examination in the old time.

45

when the weather was hot and inside the house one felt wet and sticky, the villagers, old and young, usually came out and sat in the yard, either on stone benches or on rattan chairs, or on long straw mats. The children listened to adults telling legends, adventures, or ghost stories. And a favorite pastime was usually to recite aloud the nursery rhymes. The children also did not want to miss singing along with frogs and netting fireflies under the moonlight.

My mother came to my father's family when she was only sixteen or seventeen years old. She was actually still a childlike teen, not quite ready to function in an adult's world. She luckily benefited from her mother-in-law's knowledge and love of nursery rhymes, and quickly made herself familiar with them. Moreover, my mother loved not only to recite the nursery rhymes but to hum melodies and sometimes mixed humming with singing. I heard that she hum-recited her monotonous lullaby when she was lulling my youngest brother to sleep. I heard that she hum-sang her improvised melodies as I was awaking from naps, or when she was dusting and cleaning the house, sewing clothing, washing dishes. I luckily inherited her gift and habit and hum-sing melodies often and happily, even while driving from work to home.

The monotonous lullaby, hum-recited by my mother to lull her eight children to sleep from night to dawn and which made us grow from inch to foot, was also recited by my third aunt and other mothers in the neighborhood. But this art is lost and heard no more today. The little-known lullaby that follows was a short two-sentenced verse. While lulling a baby to sleep, the verse is repeated again and again until the baby is asleep. (I guess any baby would rather fall asleep than keep hearing this short, monotonous lullaby.) Here is the verse after translation:

> *Rock and rock, grow an inch a night.*
> *Love and love, grow a foot a night.*

Although it is a simple verse, it contains a meaningful, philosophical message: Loving a baby can make it grow taller than just rocking or feeding it. So, love is necessary, like nutritious food, sunlight, clean air, and fresh water for a young, growing life. I have heard that some other mothers occasionally recited a similar verse:

> *Hushaby baby, sleep soundly;*
> *grow an inch a night.*
> *Hushaby baby, love you deeply;*
> *grow a foot a night.*

Combining my mother's two-sentence monotonous lullaby with others, I have expanded the verse text and have composed a melody to make it into a new and modified lullaby. I call this method "Seasoning the old wine with the same label but in a new bottle."

So, the bottle is changed from a small bottle to a bigger bottle. And the label is still the same: "Grow a Foot a Night." Now, let me present this new lullaby, or new wine:

Grow a Foot a Night

Rock and rock, to a dreamy sleep;
Love and love, with my heart so deep.
Rock and rock, grow an inch all right;
Love and love, grow a foot a night.

Rock and rock, cheer a dreary night;
Love and love, bring the dawn so bright.
Rock and rock, grow an inch all right;
Love and love, grow a foot a night.

Grow a foot a night.
Bring the dawn so bright.

Now, you can try to sing this melody, which is sung in my mother's tongue. Or you may try to sing it in English, based on the translation following.

Grow A Foot A Night

Text and Melody Created by Julia Lin

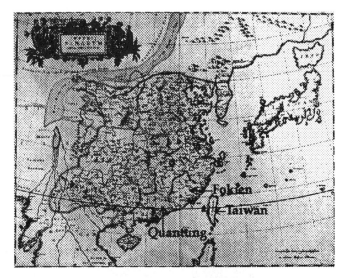

China and Taiwan in 1655

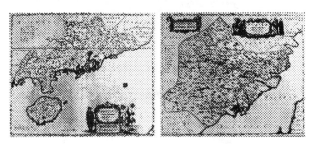

Quantung   Fokien

The Novus Atlas Sinensis (New Atlas of China), a 17th century atlas of China, was prepared by the Jesuit Priest Father Martino Martini, an Italian Jesuit who died at Hangtzhou in 1661, of the Society of Jesus and published in Amsterdam in 1655. The Atlas is part of the Special Collections of the California State University Hayward Library.

5. The Tang Mountain Souls

Who puffed the fluffy *Hundeblumen*[1] (dandelions) away so that they wandered over mountains and seas and went to seed in the evergreen island, Taiwan? Who shooed the mute swans away so that they ventured over mountains and seas and headed to breed at the vegetated lakes in Taiwan? In the old times and under tyranny, the humble people's lives were treated like dandelions growing in the wilderness, insignificant weeds easily trodden under foot. In the *Shu Jing*, the Book of Odes, one of the famous Chinese classics compiled and edited by Confucius, the sorrowfully moaning swans were compared to the wailing refugees from a chaotic state who fled to seek shelter and protection from invasion or oppression.

---

1. It refers to *Die Hundeblume* written by Wolfgang Borchert (1921-1947), a German author who died very young. He metaphorically associated the life of wilderness-growing dandelions with the life of wandering poor dogs, *Hunde*. The association was to reflect the life of prisoners who had no dignity as dandelions and dogs. Borchert was jailed as a political prisoner.

So, who was this big-mouthed, long-handed monster, who puffed away the fluffy *Hundeblumen* and shooed away the mute swans?

In 1600, China's population was more than 150 million. By 1788 it had doubled. Overpopulation caused severe food shortages that left 300 million people hungry.

The coastal provinces had their natural drawbacks—more mountains and less arable land—which were the main cause of a famine. To satisfy their hungry stomachs, the Hollos of Fokien and the Hakkas of Quantung had to venture out and to seek their own *Taur-Hwa-Yueng*,[1] or utopia.

The foreign rulers, the Manchus, allowed not even a free choice of hairdo; they shouted their sharp motto: "Keep your head or keep your hair." If one wanted to keep his head, he had to shave off the front hair and keep a pigtail in back like the Manchus. If one wanted to keep his Han hairdo with a topknot, his head would be chopped off. As an act of refusing to observe the Manchu rule of the hairdo, the Hakkas of Quantung jumped into the southern sea and fled to the South Pacific islands, and the Hollos of Fokien jumped into the eastern sea and fled to Penghus and Taiwan.

---

1. This refers to the narrative story *The Origin of the Peach Blossom*, written by the great poet Tao Yuen-ming (365-427), in which the dream place was a utopia where people lived in peace and were oblivious to the passing of time.

Lastly, Fokien had been the shipyards for naval and commercial vessels since the Chin Dynasty (221-206 B.C.) and a marine goods transportation center since the Tang Dynasty (618-907 A.D.). Owing to the very enticing advantage of good, natural harbors, the Hollos, earlier than the Hakkas, braved the deep, mad occean, risked being hanged as breakers of the restrictions on emigration, and came determinedly to the new world, Taiwan.

Although the Ching Dynasty lowered the boom on sailing overseas three times between the years 1684 and 1746, a swell in population made unavoidable a "squeeze-out" of the Hollos and the Hakkas from the mainland. Like heavy sea waves, one after another, they came to their land of dreams and planted the seeds of their Han culture while they scattered rice and vegetable seeds in the new land. In other words, to escape from the crucial reality—the booming population, there was no boom that could enclose those Hollos-Hakkas floating logs.

Why were the Manchus so sensitive and cautious about allowing overseas emigration? Because they could not risk the rise of another Tey Sian-con, whose troops in Taiwan the Manchus took twenty-two years to conquer (1661-1683). Tey Sian-con, known also as Koxinga, who was the minister of the preceding dynasty, the Ming Dynasty, defeated the Dutch to end their thirty-eight years' occupation of Taiwan and then tried to restore the Ming Dynasty on this island. Unfortunately, he died in 1662 when he was only thirty-nine years old. Tey's troops in the last battle, led by Tey's fourteen-year-old grandson, had to surrender to the Manchus because the dragon-head had gone. Tey Sian-con was a man of honor who achieved immortality by being loyal to his dynasty, defeating the Dutch, and occupying beautiful Taiwan, which eventually became an expanded living space for the Hans.

In the Tang Dynasty of a thousand years ago, the Hans had fled from northern China, Honan, to southern China, Fokien and Quantung, during the invasions by the northern foreign tribes, called barbarians at that time; the invasions ended with the fall of the Tang Dynasty. During the Tang Dynasty, the Hollo culture reached its peak in poetry and Buddhism and its art forms, and the capital, Chang-an, became a famous cosmopolitan center for trade and culture. Eight hundred years later the descendants of the Hans in Fokien (the so-called Hollos) and in Quantung (the so-called Hakkas) still called the mainland "the Tang Mountains," although twelve different dynasties had passed and they were now living in the Ching Dynasty. This strong self-identity as "Tang Souls" came instinctively, and they linked themselves with the splendid and prosperous past.

Today, the modern Hollos and Hakkas in Taiwan call their ancestors who earlier followed Tey Sian-con or later escaped from hunger or famine, or refused wearing pigtails the Deng-Swan Keks, or the Tang Mountain Souls. Those brave souls came across the Taiwan Straits sailing on leaflike small boats, floating on white billows, skipping out of black whirlpools, and believing that they were guided by their beloved goddess Ma-tzo. They left one thousand ranges of lofty mountains and ten thousand miles of mighty rivers behind. Their Odyssey-like wandering, from mainland to Taiwan, is called *Deng-Swan kuei Taiwan,* or traversing the Tang Mountains to Taiwan.

My great-great-great-great uncles Lim Tung and Lim Zuh and my great-great-great-grandfather Lim Suii were "Tang Mountain Souls, " too.

In 1760, my great-great-great-great uncles came together to Taiwan; Tung was twenty-one and Zuh was seventeen. Twenty-four years later, they mysteriously died within three years of one another; Tung died in 1784 at age 45 and Zuh died in 1787 at age 44. No papers or records show why they left their home town in Penho County, Tsan-chiu, for Taiwan, or why they died so early, in the prime of their lives. This remains a riddle for us today, but none of us will ever solve it.

Did they come to Taiwan to fill their stomachs because of mother nature's disasters—the famine or the population explosion? Or did they come to restore the Han's dignity overseas after the fatherland was occupied by the Manchus—the pigtail's knot? The first guess, having growling stomachs, seems unlikely; at least, we know that their grandmother was a daughter of the provincial Teh-Doh. The second guess, fighting against the pigtail, is basically also not likely, since their grandmother's father served in the Manchu imperial court as a Teh-Doh. Thus, they surely would not want to throw away their existing happiness. Nevertheless, there is always an exception; for example, it could be their Han blood flowed thicker than Teh-Doh's, or perhaps they were easily excited and had a sudden urge for adventure, like other naive boys.

Let me guess some more possibilities: First, they were young and curious. There was a trend, a gold rush, to travel to Taiwan at that time; they joined the masses to venture, to experience, and to expand a new life overseas. Their early deaths were just accidents, like the grand old tree being stricken by a killer lightning bolt. Next, they were full of naive dreams. As an enticing voice echoed from the other side of the strand, "This is a fairyland; people wade in gold water," they came and engaged in raw land development with high pioneering spirits. Instead of washing gold, they accidentally found and ate divine peaches at a different time and so rode on divine cranes to the fairyland of the immortals. Another guess: they were two passionate young patriots absorbed and trapped by the secret society *Ten Deh Huei*, or Heaven and Earth Society, a hush-hush group formed to overthrow the Ching Dynasty of the Manchus and restore the Ming Dynasty of the Hans; unfortunately, they died at the hands of the Ching soldiers during an uprising.

Both of these ancestors remained unmarried; there were not many Han girls in Taiwan at that time. Early in 1661, Tey Sian-con brought about one hundred thousand Tsan-chiu and Zwan-chiu men to Taiwan, but only the high-ranking officials were allowed to bring their dependents. Later, the Manchu rulers forbade the Hans to bring their dependents to Taiwan when they came to cultivate the land. The Manchus' intention was "Let them walk there, and let them die there." The Manchus wanted them to die with no posterity. Therefore, it was a world crowded with sweat-smelling strong men and lacking flower-scented, soft women. This unbalanced Yin-Yang nature was a serious social problem at that time. As a result, some Han men tied the marriage-red-flower-knot with native girls—the aborigines—but most of the proud Han men would not lower their social standing, considering it degrading at that time—it was a racial prejudice, as we say today.

As the eldest grandson of his grandmother and the eldest son of his parents, my great-great-great-grandfather did not go to Taiwan and leave his old folks behind during their lifetime. He, like all the Chinese eldest sons who had more filial responsibilities than their brothers for the old family members, stayed with them and nursed them until they were called by *Tien Kong*, God of Heaven. This traditional filial responsibility was stressed by Confucius and has been practiced since then until today. His filial piety was the best example to interpret one of the Confucian teachings: "'When your parents are living, make no far trip; if you should make it, point them a direction.'"

In 1788, twenty-eight years after his two younger brothers had left for Taiwan and had died, and his mother, the last of his old folks, had died in this same year, he came with his wife and three teenage sons to Go-dun-lei, a neighboring village of Parasol Tree Village, to manage the property that his two brothers had left behind. Nine years later he passed away naturally in Go-dun-lei. He was sixty-one years old, but his wife, Nah Sham, lived twenty-three years longer until the age of eighty-one. She moved with her three sons to Parasol Tree Village in 1815.

Today, in 1999, some two hundred years later, the modern Hollo and Hakka descendants, whether in Taiwan or worldwide, see the prosperity of the island that has evolved from a desolate, primitive land to a world-class, high-technology-based, economic miracle island; without hesitation, everyone has to acknowledge that the swan song, in concert with the diligence, the frugality, the calluses, the tears, and the sweat, and sung by the Tang Mountain Souls two centuries ago, was the cornerstone of this miracle. Kudos to you—the Tang Mountain Souls!

A picture of Pi Kan is placed in the altar of the Lim clan temple.

6. The No-Heart Vegetable

Speaking of Chinese surnames, one asks: "How many surnames are there?" Although it is a simple question, the answer is indefinite since most of the Chinese are still apt to answer: "There are a hundred family names." This is the answer typically given by most Chinese since the word "hundred," semantically, implies large numbers in Chinese. However, when they use "hundred" to imply an uncertain large quantity, they do not know the real answer is actually traced back through a time tunnel of two thousand years to the Han Dynasty. In fact, today there are more than ten thousand Chinese surnames.

The following figures show the statistical records of the surnames that developed during the epochs in history, including a census in Taiwan and a recent study in Beijing, China:

- Han Dynasty (206 B.C.-220 A.D.) = 130
- Tang Dynasty (618-907) = 193

- Sung Dynasty (960-1279) = 2,302
- Yuan Dynasty (1279-1367) = 3,736
- Ming Dynasty (1368-1644) = 9, 177
- A census in Taiwan in 1978 = 1,694
  (Only within this island nation)
- A study in China in 1997 = 11,969

The character for the surname "Lim 林" is literally composed of two juxtaposing forms of the character for "tree 木." Clearly, you can see that it is in plural form—two trees—so it bears the meaning of "woods."

Lim is phonetically sounded in Fokienese, or Taiwanese, and said by the Hollos. In Mandarin, the official language, it is pronounced as Lin, which is familiar in the Western world. The pronounciation as Lum or Lam is Cantonese and is said by the Hakkas. My ancestors originally came from Fokien to Taiwan, so Fokienese (Taiwanese) is the spoken language in my family. To honor my parents, I use their native tongue, Taiwanese, in this book to refer to the names and the places that were familiar to them and were phonetically spoken by them.

The ramification of the family name Lim, from ancient days to today and from northern China to southern China, has grown denser and thicker as time has passed. Increasing prosperity can be seen by the merging of other names into its stem: In 770 B.C., in the Chou Dynasty, the posterity of Ji Lim-kai, the second son of Emperor Ping, joined with the Lims because their father's name started with Lim. In 600 B.C., during the Spring-Autumn Epoch, the family name Shir, snake, changed from Shir to Lim because the family thought that the snake should return to the woods. In 500 A.D., during the South-North Epoch, a foreign tribe named Chiou Lim, the hilly trees, or the wooded hills, admired the fame of the prosperous Lims and changed their family name to Lim. Because of all these factors, today in Taiwan Lim as a family name is second only to the most popular one—Cheng.

The origin of the surname Lim goes back 3,133 years to Lim Kien,[1] upon whom the surname Lim was conferred by Emperor Wu (reigned from 1122 to 1114 B.C.) of the Chou Dynasty to honor Lim Kien's father Pi Kan, the uncle and vice premier of Emperor Zou (reigned from 1154 to 1121 B.C.), the last ruler of the Ying Dynasty. Emperor Zou was so notorious for his killing orgies that he was named "the Tyrant" and has been reviled ever since.

It is said that Pi Kan, because of his faithful and sincere advice, was executed by having his heart gouged out by his own heartless, cruel nephew, Emperor Zou. Pi Kan's advice was, "Be industrious in the work of the state and have compassion for the people." It seemed this piece of advice

---

1. Asians place the surname before the first (given) name.

grated on the tyrant's ears. Pi Kan's wife, who was pregnant at that time, ran for her life and hid herself under two giant trees in the wilderness, where she delivered their son, Lim Kien. Thus, Pi Kan's family line carried on.

Emperor Wu, whose father was one of the four large feudal lords of the tyrant Emperor Zou, overturned the Ying Dynasty and named his dynasty the Chou Dynasty. In recognition of Pi Kan's loyalty and sacrifice to the preceding dynasty, Emperor Wu in 1120 B.C. conferred a hereditary high official rank "Ching Da Fu" along with feudal estates in Poh-lin (Hopeh province today) to Pi Kan's two-year-old son and bestowed the family name "Lim" on him because of the place—under two trees— where the boy had been born. (Another story says the name is derived from the place name Chang Lim, long trees, where the boy was hidden during the chaos.) So, Pi Kan's posthumous son was then named Lim Kien. Kien stands for strong, solid, durable, thriving, and stalwart. This was the wish of Emperor Wu for Lim Kien, to see him grow and become a stalwart man who should be as strong and solid as a thriving tree.

Pi Kan was buried fifteen miles northwest of the Wei Hwei prefecture in Honan. People later found a bunch of no-heart vegetable,[2] featuring a hollow stalk, growing near his tomb; therefore, it became a custom, not widely adopted, to plant no-heart vegetable at the sides of the tombs. It

---

2. The no-heart vegetable is a species of water convolvulus.

became a token of Lim. From this you can see that people did not want him to die, so they transformed him into a vegatable, showing that his spirit has never died.

On a "Tomb-Sweeping Day" in my teens, I saw a lot of these vegetables growing in a water planting bed in front of my great-grandparents' and grandparents' tombs in the cemetery in Parasol Tree Village. The Tomb-Sweeping Day was actually called Ching Ming, Clean and Clear, by the Chinese. The day is one of the 24 solar periods in a year and falls on April 5 or 6. On this day people visit and clean their ancestral tombs and also worship and remember their ancestors.

Confucius and many emperors in different epochs honored and glorified Pi Kan, each in his own way. The italic number at the end of each listed item shows the total years since the death of Pi Kan.

1. In 1109 B.C., Emperor Wu of the Chou Dynasty resealed Pi Kan's tomb and bestowed a bronze disk with an engraved inscription. (*13*)

2. Confucius (551-479 B.C.) presented an epitaph written in an ancient calligraphic style, a seal style. (*600*)

3. In 471-477 A.D., Emperor Hsiao-wen of the Northern Wei Dynasty built the base of the tomb. (*1,590*)

4. In 627, Emperor Tai-tzong of the Tang Dynasty conferred a posthumous title "Loyalty and Martyrdom." (*1,749*)

5. In 1056, the imperial censor Lim Yeh asked to return home to honor and sweep Pi Kan's tomb, and Emperor Jen-tzong not only consented but also presented the sealed inscription "Loyalty and Piety" to honor Pi Kan and his outstanding descendant, Lim Yeh, the imperial censor. (2,178)

6. In 1522, Emperor Shih-tzong of the Ming Dynasty reconstructed the tomb; since then there have been a total of ten remodeling constructions. (2,644)

7. In 1736, the emperor Cheng-long himself led hundreds of the imperial courtiers to worship Pi Kan and inscribed rhymes on the tablet. (2,858)

Thus, Pi Kan's loyalty has been touched by emperors and the people in every epoch until today—more than three thousand years later. A picture of him is placed in the altar of the Lim clan temple of Parasol Tree Village so that he may be worshipped as the father of the Lims and to commemorate his patriotic virtue as a role model for generations to follow.

The tragedy of Pi Kan's life is well narrated in a classical novel of Chinese gods and heroes: *Fong Sheng Pang*, or *The List of Deific Heroes*, in which the author Lu Hsi-hsing of the Ming Dynasty (1368-1644) depicts the fall of the 600-year-old Shang-Ying Dynasty[3] that is caused by the tyrannical rule of Emperor Zou. In this dramatically developed story, a faithful and sincere uncle, a subject, is framed by his vicious nephew-emperor under the influence of the emperor's crafty concubine Dah-chi, whose evil deeds can be compared with those of Lady Macbeth of William Shakespeare's (1564-1616) play *Macbeth*. Lady Macbeth is described as viperous as a serpent under the flowers; Dah-chi is cast as a thousand-year-old bewitching fox in a form of a human being and has seductive charm.

The novel contains a total of 100 chapters, but for the sake of brevity here I translate only partly the first six chapters and Chapter 26. From these excerpted, translated chapters you will see how cruel and muddled-headed Emperor Zou is, and how Pi Kan is framed by Zou's plotting, vicious concubine Dah-chi.

---

3. The 17th emperor, Pan Kuen (reigned from 1401 to 1372 B.C.), changed the dynasty title from Shang to Ying.

Chapter 1: Emperor Zou Lights Incense at Ni Wa Temple

One day Emperor Di-yee led all his courtiers outside to appreciate the beauty and the fragrance of the peonies in his imperial garden. Suddenly, a rotten beam of a cloud-high pavilion toppled and fell. Emperor Di-yee's third son, Prince Sou, stretched out his strong arms in time to catch the falling beam and then restored the pavilion by replacing the rotten piece with a new one. Therefore, Emperor Di-yee, with the agreement of his premier and statesmen, appointed Prince Sou to be heir prince and settled him in the East Quad of the palace. Years later when Emperor Di-yee passed away, Prince Sou was crowned as Emperor Zou in Chaokge, the capital.

Emperor Zou's imperial court was well formed. It included the following members: a judicious and experienced grand counselor who had served two previous emperors and led a group of wise and prudent statemen. Two majestic military generals led four large feudatories: East, West, South, North; each feudatory had its own feudal lord, who led 200 garrison troops in defense. Three gracious and quiet palace quads: the Middle Quad as the empress Jiang's, the West Quad as the cuncubine Huang's, and the Shinching Quad as the cuncubine Yang's. Emperor Zou was the luckiest emperor ever, enjoying blossoms and fruits without toiling.

One day during the morning court session, the premier Shang Jong informed Zou that the next day, the 15th day of the third moon, was the birthday of the goddess Ni Wa and advised Zou to go to her temple to light incense and to pray for the granting of ample blessings.

After Emperor Zou finished incensing, he glanced over the hall and was impressed by the grandeur of the splendid, gold-embellished temple of Ni Wa. Suddenly, a fast-blowing wind rolled up the curtain and disclosed her portrait. "A real beauty who can be only found in heaven," he thought. He was infatuated, head over heels, and couldn't help but write a poem on the wall praising her grand temple in its steep mountain setting and her beauty as far beyond that of a pear blossom in rain and a peony in mist. He wished that she were a living creature so that he could bring her home to serve him. Immediately, the premier advised Emperor Zou to erase the poem, because it was impertinent and could invite trouble, but the arrogant emperor ignored his advice.

When the goddess Ni Wa came back from her birthday feast, she was insulted and furious to see the poem on the wall. She opened a golden calabash bottle, from which came a thread of white light and a forty-foot-long silk flag, the evil-spirit-inducing flag, hanging in five colors with a thousand reflecting rays on top. After several rushing sounds of wind, all the evil spirits appeared and waited for their mission. The goddess Ni Wa dismissed them all except for three sinful evil spirits—a thousand-year-old fox, a nine-headed pheasant, and a jade *pi-pa*, a lute. The secret mission given to them by Ni Wa was to slip into the Ying court, and not only to bewitch Emperor Zou and cause his dynasty to fall, but also to help the future emperor of the new dynasty to be born. Literally, they were instructed to destroy and finish the 600-year-old Ying Dynasty. However, the most important thing, Ni Wa emphasized was that the evil spirits should harm no living thing. If they accomplished their task, their sinful souls would be cleansed and they would be transformed into mortal beings.

After seeing Ni Wa's portrait in her temple, the emperor became a captive to her beauty and had no more desire for his empress and the two cuncubines. The grand counselor was sent to subdue an uprising in the northern sea and was not in court; predestinedly arranged by Ni Wa, Emperor Zou accepted the fatal suggestion of two wicked officials to recruit beauties from the whole land.

Chapter 2: *The Uprising of Su Fu of Jih-chou Fiefdom*

Emperor Zou asked the rulers of his four fiefdoms to choose a hundred girls from each town to fill his court, but the plan was stopped by his prudent premier. Later, however, the two wicked officials told the emperor that Su Fu, one of his eight hundred feudal officials, had a sixteen-year-old daughter named Su Dah-chi who was a heavenly beauty. When Emperor Zou requested that the daughter be sent to his court, Su Fu refused to comply; instead, he led an uprising to protest the emperor's order.

The two feudal lords, Ji Chang in the west and Tsung Ho-fu in the north, were ordered by the emperor to quell the uprising by Su Fu. Ji Chang believed using military force to control rebels would not be wise, since war would have only a negative omen; besides, he believed Su Fu to be a longtime loyal official. Tsung Ho-fu, however, chose to use force and led his troops against Su Fu. In the end Tsung Ho-fu and his son were defeated by Su Chuan-chung, son of Su Fu, but luckily, they both finally escaped safely after a long chase.

Chapter 3: *Ji Chang Solves a Dilemma: Presenting Dah-chi*

When the fierce Tsung He-fu, brother of the north feudal lord Tsung Ho-fu, came to rescue his brother and nephew, he defeated Su Chuan-chung, the son of Su Fu, who then was imprisoned and sent to the capital. But then one of Su Fu's subordinates performed black magic to cause the arrest of Tsung He-fu. When Su Fu met Tsung He-fu, he was not only very courteous to Tsung but blamed himself for making the world a mess. Tsung He-fu was very moved by Su Fu's kindness, and they became friends.

The west feudal lord Ji Chang sent no troops but instead a letter to Su Fu, in which Ji asked Su not to use weapons against the emperor; instead, Ji wrote, Su should present his daughter to the emperor and maintain the proper feudal manner toward the emperor. Ji presented three good reasons. First, the daughter would receive favors from the emperor, the father would enjoy the position of a prominent guest in the concubine's quad, and the whole family would become kin to the emperor and live in affluence. Second, the feudal state of Jih-chou would be at peace and no house would be disturbed. Third, the common people would not suffer from chaos and the soldiers would not die in wars. Su Fu showed the letter to Tsung He-fu, and they both were enlightened and agreed with Ji Chang's judgment.

Chapter 4: *The Fox Kills Dah-chi at the Eng-chou Post House*

Su Fu himself escorted his elegantly dressed daughter Dah-chi to the imperial court, accompanied by 3,000 horsemen and 500 servants. The first night on the road at the Eng-chou post house, as everyone was resting, a gust of wind blew out the candles. Su Fu whipped out his sword and ran into Dah-chi's chamber and asked if she were all right. He was relieved when she answered that nothing had disturbed her. But actually, at the moment of the strong gust of wind, the thousand-year-old fox had sucked Dah-chi's soul out of her body and slid her own evil body into Dah-chi's. So the innocent Su Dah-chi existed no more; she was dead. Now, Dah-chi was really a thousand-year-old enchanted fox, who had the outward appearance of the innocent Su Dah-chi but possessed an evil nature.

Upon arriving in the imperial court, Dah-chi was called to meet Emperor Zou on his throne with his courtiers lined along both sides. Everyone acknowledged and admired Dah-chi's beauty. Emperor Zou was captivated immediately by her charming manner and settled her in the Sousen Quad of the palace. The emperor not only reinstated Su Fu in his post but also increased his compensation and gave him a good reward. Having such a lustful emperor, the premier and all the courtiers couldn't help but sigh. The Sousen Quad had a big celebration for three days and three nights. In the following months, the emperor was often absent during court sessions.

73

Chapter 5: *Yun Chung-tze Presents a Sword against Charms*

A thousand-year-old Taoist, a divine named Yun Chung-tze (Son of Cloud), lived at Jade Pillar Cave on Chung-nan Mountain. On a leisurely day on the way to gather herbs, he saw the evil thousand-year-old fox promenading in the palace. As a merciful Taoist, he thought that he had the responsibility to tell the emperor to get rid of this evil soul at once or he would regret it later. When the emperor asked him how to get rid of the fox, the Taoist presented him with a pine sword from his herb-flower basket. Then, he told the emperor that the pine sword should be hung above the palace-dividing tower.

On the same afternoon, the emperor did not see Dah-chi waiting for him at the palace-dividing tower where she usually welcomed him when he came to the Sousen Quad. Instead, he was told that Dah-chi was very sick and couldn't come to greet him. Later she told him that she got sick because she saw a pine sword hanging high on the palace-dividing tower. Now, the emperor thought that he had been deceived by Yun Chung-tze, the Taoist divine, and ordered the pine sword burned immediately. Burning the pine sword was equivalent to burning down the Ying Dynasty, so the evil power took over the dynasty and Dah-chi held sway again. All these events were actually planned and predestined by the goddess Ni Wa.

Chapter 6: *The Cruel Tyrant Builds Burning Pillars*

The Taoist divine did not leave the capital right away; he saw that the pine sword had been burned and the evil light was shining in the palace again. He was so sad about the emperor's foolishness in not accepting his warning. The divine wrote a verse with twenty-four characters on the outside wall of the astronomical observator before he left the capital for his divine abode: "An evil spirit dirties the palace; a virtuous saint is planted in the west land. The capital will be bloody in just seven years."

After reading the verse, the aged, loyal minister of the astronomical observatory, who had also served the previous two emperors, sincerely tried to advise the emperor about the evil spirit hiding in the palace, as related by the Taoist Yun Chung-tze, but he lost his head as a consequence of his advice. There was also a rumor going around that an evil spirit was hiding somewhere in the palace. As the wind of the rumor blew into Dah-chi's ears, she made the emperor build a line of twenty bronze burning pillars to burn anyone who tried to tell the emperor to shun her or who said openly that Dah-chi was an evil enchantress.

Sincere advice is often grating on the ears; a lustful mind easily blinds the eyes. So it was with Emperor Zou, who had neither ears nor eyes for anything but Dah-chi's charm. And the cruel burning pillars had melted away any sincere loyalty. For this reason, the aged, very disappointed premier, who had served two former emperors, asked to resign and returned to his home village. Later, Pi Kan was promoted from vice premier to premier.

Chapter 26: Dah-chi Plots to Frame Pi Kan

On a snow-drifting winter day, while the emperor and Dah-chi were banqueting on the Deer Terrace-Tower, Pi Kan presented Emperor Zou a foxskin robe. The emperor was very pleased with Pi Kan's thoughtfulness and tried it on right away. Hidden behind a curtain, Dah-chi was greatly pained to see that the robe was made out of her kindred, and she determined to seek revenge. She said to the emperor: "Your Majesty has the body of a sublime dragon; wearing such a robe made of foxskin surely brings disgrace upon you." The emperor agreed with her and put the robe away in a vault.

To start her evil plot, she asked help from her fellow fox, Hsi-mei, and let her flirt with the emperor and tempt him to pleasure. Henceforth, the emperor ignored state affairs and was harder for his subjects to reach, even though the east feudal lord Jiang Wen-fan had deployed troops to attack the borders.

One morning, as Emperor Zou, Dah-chi, and Hsi-mei were having their breakfast on the Deer Terrace-Tower, Dah-chi suddenly screamed and fell to the ground. The emperor was very frightened to see Dah-chi's face turn purple with her two eyes closed tight and her mouth spitting watery blood. He asked: "My dear wife, you have stayed with me for years and have never been sick. Why today do you suffer from such a terrible illness?" Hsi-mei nodded her head and sighed: "My sister suffers a relapse of an old ailment." Emperor Zou asked: "Hsi-mei beauty, how do you know that my wife has this old ailment?" Hsi-mei answered: "In the old days when we were still maidens, sister Dah-chi used to suffer from heart disease. There was a doctor named Chang Yuen in Jih-chou who prescribed a marvelous soup—made from of a fried delicate heart—that cured it." The emperor ordered: "Call in the doctor Chang Yuen of Jih-chou." Hsi-mei replied: "Your Majesty is wrong! What a great distance from Chaokge to Jih-chou! To go there and back requires more than a month. If there is a delay, it would be regretted. Unless we secure the soup locally, she will die."

Emperor Zou asked: "Who has a delicate heart?" Hsi-mei answered: "I was an apprentice to a master and learned well the psychic arts." Emperor Zou happily asked her to practice the arts right away. This vicious fox bent her fingers once or twice, then said: "The only person with a delicate heart is the most prominent official among all. I am afraid that he will not be willing to save the empress' life." Emperor Zou asked: "Who is he? Hurry!" Hsi-mei answered: "Only the premier Pi Kan has a delicate heart with seven pores of intellectual capacity." Emperor Zou said: "Pi Kan is not only the throne's uncle, but also a clan member of the same family tree; therefore, he shouldn't refuse lending a heart to save my wife's life. Hurry! Call in Pi Kan." The messenger Ching flew to the premier's mansion.

Six edicts were sent, one after another, to summon Pi Kan. Pi Kan was suspicious and wondered why he received six edicts in such a hurry. So, he asked Ching and was told what had happened that morning during breakfast and also about lending his heart to save the empress' life.

Pi Kan repeated what he heard from the messenger to his wife and asked her to take good care of their adopted son and observe the family rule—be faithful to the country. Both were in tears as he bade farewell. His son cried and said: "Father, don't worry. I just remember what Jiang Tzu-ya[4] said last time that he read an ill fate in your face, and when he left an envelope for you in the study and stressed 'Open it when in a dilemma to save your life.'" Pi Kan now remembered the envelope and rushed to the study and took the envelope from under the inkstone. He read it and then said: "Give me a fire!" He poured water into a bowl, burned the "Tzi-ya" charm, let the ashes fall into the water-

---

4. Jiang Tzu-ya is the main character in this book and is cast as a Taoist; at the end, he helps Emperor Wu found the Chou Dynasty.

bowl, and drank it. Then he dressed in his court robe and rode away at a gallop toward the palace gate.

The messenger disclosed the emperor's idea of lending Pi Kan's heart to save the empress' life, which terrified all the courtiers and the people. General Huang and other officials waited for Pi Kan at the palace gate. As Pi Kan rode by on horseback, they followed him to the palace hall. Immediately, Pi Kan was called up to the Deer Terrace-Tower. The emperor said: "My wife has had a sudden heart attack and only a delicate heart can cure it. Uncle, you have such a fine heart, so I want to borrow a lobe of it to save her life. I will give you great credit for it." Pi Kan said: "What is the heart?" Emperor Zou said: "It is the heart that is in uncle's belly." Pi Kan replied angrily: "The heart is the main part of a body. It is hidden behind the lung and sits between six lobes and two auricles. It is threatened by a hundred sort of evils; once it is attacked, it dies immediately. If the heart is kind, the hands and feet respond benignly; if the heart is unkind, the hands and feet respond malignly. The heart is the soul of all creatures and the root of the movement of the four limbs. If my heart is hurt, how could I survive!? If I died only as a conscientious subject, it might not be worth pitying as a loss; however, the state is ruined if capable and virtuous men are exterminated. Now, you, the fatuous emperor, listen to the words of an evil enchantress and grant such a heart-gouging disaster upon me. I am sure that if Pi Kan lives, the throne lives, and if Pi Kan exists, the state exists!"

Emperor Zou said: "Uncle, your words are wrong! I just want to borrow a lobe of your heart. It is not a big deal; why do you need to say so much?" Pi Kan shouted: "Fatuous emperor! You indulge in the pleasures of wine and women and are as muddle-headed as a dog! I would die if you gouged out a lobe of my heart. I am innocent and have not committed a crime that deserves gouging out the heart. For what, why do I have to suffer this disaster?" Emperor Zou said in anger: "If the emperor asks his subject to die, he should die; otherwise, he is not faithful! To argue with me, your emperor, in my tower, means you lack the virtue of a subject! You don't obey my order. Soldiers! Take him away and gouge out his heart!" Pi Kan shouted angrily: "Dah-chi, the bitch! I will not be ashamed when I see the ancestral emperors in the underworld!" Then, he shouted: "Anyone, left or right, give me a sword!" The emperor's page tossed him a sword. Pi Kan caught it and held it in his hand; he looked toward the ancestral shrine and bowed eight times and said in tears: "My ancestral emperor Chen Tarng, how could one have known that Ying would end the throne of Chen Tarng at the 28th generation! It is not my unfaithfulness!" Then, he loosened his belt and exposed his body; he stabbed himself in the navel and opened up his belly, but there was no bleeding. Pi Kan grabbed his heart from under his opened belly, threw it on the ground, then dressed in silence, and came down from the tower with his face shining in pale gold. All the courtiers waited anxiously outside the hall and criticized the misrule of the state; then, they heard rushing footsteps coming from inside. General Huang was glad to see Pi Kan come out and asked him how things were going. Pi Kan lowered his head, with his face still shining in pale gold, and said no words but quickly passed them by. He crossed the Nine Dragon Bridge and walked out of the palace gate. Then, his page attended him as he mounted his horse. He rode toward the north gate and was soon out of sight.

General Huang saw that Pi Kan was very depressed, so he sent Huang Ming and Chou Chi to follow the premier. Pi Kan galloped off at full speed, sounding like sweeping wind. After riding about five to seven miles, he saw a woman with a bamboo basket in hand who cried: "No-heart vegetables!" Pi Kan stopped suddenly as he heard her. He asked her: "What is a no-heart vegetable?" The woman answered: "I am selling no-heart vegetables." Pi Kan asked: "How would it be, if a person had no heart?" The woman answered quickly and firmly: "If a person had no heart, he should die." Pi Kan screamed loudly and fell off his horse; at the same time, blood from his belly splashed all over the dust. The woman saw what was happening and fled away in fright. As Huang Ming and Chou Chi rode up, they saw Pi Kan dying under his horse, face up, his robe stained red by the blood on the ground. They both were puzzled at such a sight.

Postscript:

The charm left by Jiang Tzu-ya that Pi Kan read: "Burn the charm in a bowl of water and drink it to protect the five internal organs—the heart, liver, spleen, lungs, and kidneys." This charm-water enabled Pi Kan to step down from the tower, walk out of the palace gate, and ride out of the north gate. But the charm was broken by the curse "He should die" from the woman selling no-heart vegetables, who was really Dah-chi in disguise.

A art work combining a part of frescoes to the photo of the temple found on the wall in the main training hall of the Shaolin temple.

The Budda Da Mo, the founder of the Shaolin Kungfu, stood on a reed to float across the river.

7. An Unsung Hero

Do you remember that in the previous chapter entitled *The Emperor and the Parasol Trees* I told you about the emperor Cheng-long's ten battles, including the one waged to quell the rebellion in Taiwan? The rebellion's locale was in Dai-li-khit, and it was the only battlefield outside the mainland, or let me say outside Central Asia but inside his own imperial land. The tenth battle was fought to annihilate the members of the Heaven and Earth Society, and to capture its leader Lim Sung-bun, who lived in Dai-li-khit and who was a reputable townsman of nearby Parasol Tree Village.

Lim Sung-bun's life and story is mentioned or heard no more today. He is a long forgotten figure in the Chinese history, although he lived just about two hundred years ago. Here, let me introduce you the Lim Sung-bun Event along with its interesting background; besides, I want to redress a miscarriage of justice and give him a position in the modern Chinese history.

In the mid-1600s, the Heaven and Earth Society, known also as Hong Mung Huei, or by its nickname, the Red Gang, was an undercover society. The society was dedicated to overthrowing the Manchu regime and restoring the Ming Dynasty. It became the antecessor of Hsing Chung Huei and Tung Meng Huei, founded by Dr. Sun Yat-sen at Honolulu in 1894 and at Tokyo in 1905, respectively. After overthrowing the Manchu regime in 1911, Dr. Sun Yat-sen, father of the Republic of China, founded Kuomintang, the Nationalist Party. Kuomintang is today the executive party of the Republic of China in Taiwan.

Who created the Heaven and Earth Society? There are no complete historical records about it. However, there are several controversial versions. One says that it was created by Tey Sian-con himself. Another says: "No, it was created by one of the military tacticians of Tey's, Chen Jung-hwa, who secretly formed self-protection troops after Tey's power surrendered to the Manchus." Hong Mung's own Sea Bottom, the Secret Documents, said that it was created by the five surviving Buddhist monastery monks out of the original 128 of South Shaolin Temple of Fokien, who had helped the emperor Kang-hsi turn back the troops of the Tsar at the Yakutsk. But, after the battle, 123 monks were butchered by the Ching troops, although they had given meritorious service to the Ching Dynasty. Because of this ungrateful act—returning evil for good, Chen Jing-nan, a brilliant military strategist of Tey's, was able to unite the surviving five monks and added five horse traders (five generals sent by Tey Sian-con, according to another source) to form an alliance, naming it *Ten Dih Huei* or literally Heaven Earth Society, and to deploy the troops to many locales to wait for a chance to take action.[1]

It is widely recognized that the Tsan-chiu and Zwan-chiu areas were the cradles of the Heaven and Earth Society. But whose hands rocked these cradles? At the end of the Ming Dynasty, many sea pirates threatened the lives and plundered the possesions of the coastal people of Tsan-chiu and Zwan-chiu. This dangerous situation produced a strong need to form a structure for self-protection. Next, the perpetual fighting dragged on because of a long-harbored, narrow-minded grudge, a typical weakness among the Chinese. The fighting included Tsan-chiu versus Zwan-chiu, South Village versus North Village, Family East versus Family West. Last, to protect from sudden, unexpected attacks, including flying fists and stones, many similar protective units were needed to guard against mobs or gangsters. These self-defense units were the embryonic forces that made these two places the cradles for the Heaven and Earth Society. When Chen Jing-nan formed the underworld society, all these structures spontaneously joined in and were absorbed by it.

---

1. *Narrating the Ching Dynasty in Detail* (I) by Li Dong-fong, page 230.

One cannot deny the historical contribution and the great influence that the Heaven and Earth Society had prior to the overthrow of the Ching Dynasty by Tung Meng Huei. To say it more correctly, the activities resulting in the overthrow of the Ching Dynasty actually started during the mid-1600s against the second emperor, Kang-hsi, and continued through 1911 against the last emperor, Xuan-tung. The anti-Ching movements spanned about 250 years and eight emperors, to each of which the Heaven and Earth Society at first gave a hand and then later strongly supported. The members of the society helped Tung Meng Huei to overthrow the Ching Dynasty and found the Republic of China. Earlier the society had supported Hung Hsiu-chuan of the Heavenly Kingdom of Peace (1851-1864) during the rebellion against the Ching government. Later, the society figured in two incidents involving Tzu I-kui and Lim Sung-bun in Taiwan, whose stories will follow later in this chapter.

Since the Heaven and Earth Society was a secret organization, certain jargon and gestures were used between members to communicate and identify each other. To join the society and to become sworn brothers and sisters of the eternal brotherhood and sisterhood, one had to go through a formal ritual, in which one made vows while kneeling and lighting incense before the altar of loyalty and virtue of the deified heros and then repeating the pledge after the senior members, sentence by sentence: "I bow to Heaven and accept it as our father. I bow to Earth and accept it as our mother. I bow to the Sun and accept it as our brother. I bow to the Moon and accept it as our sister. We knot together the Heaven and Earth Society. We, sworn brothers and sisters of the four seas [the world], unite heart-to-heart and work arm in arm to resist the Ching Dynasty and resume the Ming Dynasty." To prove his or her loyalty and virtue, one pricked his or her finger and collected the red blood in a bowl of clear water and then drank it.[2]

There is another version of the ritual: Instead of pricking one's finger, a chicken's head was chopped off. That meant after taking the oath before the altar, one should keep his promise; otherwise, the chicken, the sacrifice, would come back and take his life as a consequence of the betrayal.

Bowing to the sun and the moon bears great significance. The character "Ming" (Brightness) is actually made from two separate characters: the sun and the moon, with the character for the sun on the left and the character for the moon on the right, both side by side, joined together. Bowing to the sun and the moon thus symbolized paying homage to the Ming Dynasty. "Brightening the universe" was loudly used as the founding slogan of the Ming Dynasty, and it hinted that the universe was brightened by the sun and the moon. That is why, in my opinion, the initiates made a pledge to the sun and the moon as brothers and sisters to identify themselves as loyal and virtuous subjects of the Ming Dynasty.

---

2. *The Black Whirlpool* by Yau Jia-wen

Now, let me tell about the South Shaolin Temple, whose five monks joined the Heaven and Earth Society to fight the Ching government to avenge the murder of 123 of their fellow monks. The temple was used as a base for anti-Ching movements during the early Ching Dynasty, and it also played an important role in the Lim Sung-bun's uprising. Here are some facts about its history, its uncommonly fascinating story based on the text by Lu Fui-feng[3] and combined with my own research.

Shaolin Temple is a Zen Buddhist center that has been famous for centuries for the martial arts Kungfu. There are two Shaolin Temples, North Shaolin Temple and South Shaolin Temple. North Shaolin Temple is located in the Song Mountains in central China, in Dengfung County of Hebei Province. This range of mountains comprises two parts: the eastern Taishi Mountain and and the western Shaoshi Mountain. Shaoshi Mountain resembles a lotus, so the natives call it the "Ring of Nine Lotus Flowers." Shaolin Temple is named after the bamboo grove (lin) of Shaoshi Mountain.

North Shaolin Temple was built in 495 by Emperor Hsiao-wen of the Northern Wei Dynasty for an Indian monk named Buddha. Twenty-five years later, there came another Indian monk, Bodhidharma, who, famous for his "light-body" kungfu, crossed the Yangtze River on a reed and founded the Shaolin school of the martial arts. After

---

3. *"Trademarks" of the Chinese (II):* Bodhidharma, Kungfu, Shaolin Temple

spending nine years sitting and facing the wall in Zen-style meditation, during which he observed and was inspired by the fighting movement of animals, Bodhidharma developed China's first kungfu, which is known as the "five styles of Shaolin." The five styles are patterned after the crane, the serpent, the dragon, the tiger, and the leopard.

Because South Shaolin Temple burned down and was lost, there has been much controversy about where it was actually located. For a long period, people believed it was located in Putien County of Fokien Province either on Mount Jiolain (Nine Lotus Mountain), or on Mount Jiolong (Nine Dragons Mountain). Jiolain and Jiolong made the matter more confusing because they sound similar if Jiolong is pronounced in a local dialect. But there is no Mount Jiolain nor any record of South Shaolin Temple in Putien County. There is a Mount Jiolong, which made people believe that South Shaolin Temple was located in Putien. Some elders said that it stood on the coast in Zwan-chiu. *The Zwan-chiu Chronicle* clearly recorded that there was a Shaolin Temple on Mount Jiolain, which was built by Emperor Hsi-tzung of the Tang Dynasty during his reign in 874-880. The burning of the temple, in my opinion, could be one of the many episodes in the annihilation of the members of the Heaven and Earth Society of the Manchus.

"Mount Jiolain" was actually the password used by the members of the secret society; it really referred to the "Ring of Nine Lotus Flowers" of Shaoshi Mountain, where the original Shaolin Temple stands in the Song Mountain range.

In February 1997, the *World Journal*, a Chinese daily newspaper in Millbrae, California, published an exciting article saying that the China News Agency reported finding the ruins of South Shaolin Temple in Shaolin Natural Village, in Shin-ning District, Dong-chang Town, Fu-ching City, Fokien Province. The article also noted that both the research and the excavation, in progress since 1993, have resulted in the unearthing of written documents and many objects, including 236 pieces of Lotus-shaped seats, some 20 porcelain bowls bearing the characters "Shao Lin," slabs from stone bridges carved with the characters "Shao Lin," and several big stone urns. This report provided the answer to a mystery that has puzzled people for two hundred years.

Next, let me describe the anti-Ching movement in Taiwan. Long before the uprising by Lim Sung-bun, several smaller ones had already been put down. One of them occurred in 1721, during the 60th year of the reign of Kang-hsi. The uprising was led by Tzu I-kui, joined by a force of almost three hundred thousand at Luo-han Gate in southern Taiwan. Tzu I-kui was a member of the Heaven and Earth Society and had been an official of the Ming Dynasty. After its fall, he dedicated his life to the anti-

Ching movement. He served under Tey Sian-con's troops for years until Tey's grandson surrendered to the Ching government. He then lived in seclusion for decades as a duck farmer in Luo-han Gate, concealing himself behind his ducks, which was the best shelter for the activities of the secret society. He kept his connections with those loyal to the Ming Dynasty, persuading like-minded fellows and worldly monks to join him in the effort. After occupying Taiwan for three months, his forces were overthrown and he was taken to Beijing for execution.

There were two more uprisings, one in 1732, in the 10th year of the reign of Yung-tseng, and the other in 1770, in the 35th year of the reign of Cheng-long. But neither was as earthshaking as the one led by Lim Sung-bun sixteen years later, which has been said to have "startled the heavens and moved the earth." To quell this uprising, the emperor Cheng-long sent more than twenty thousand soldiers across the Taiwan Straits. After this battle, the longest of his ten battles, his dynasty crumbled from prosperity into decay.

Lim Sung-bun was born in 1757, in the 22nd year of the reign of Cheng-long, in Pen-ho County, Tsan-chiu, Fokien of the mainland. When he was sixteen years old, his wealthy parents moved to Taiwan and settled in Dai-li-khit, a small town adjacent to Parasol Tree Village. As an adult, he was generous and philanthropic and was recognized as the local leader in all social activities. Because of danger from continued fighting caused by long-harbored grudges between the prominent families in the nearby towns, he recruited and raised his own troops and stockaded his residence for protection.

As the leader of the Heaven and Earth Society, Lim Sung-bun is believed to have been associated with the visit to Taiwan of Yen Yen of Pen-ho County, Tsan-chiu. Yen Yen, a monk of South Shaolin Temple and an active member of this underground society, came to visit Lim Sung-bun in 1783, in the 48th year of the reign of Cheng-long. After his visit, a stream of people, including the surviving participants of the failed uprisings, came to visit him and to join the society. News of this dark society spread rapidly from mouth to mouth, and in its increasing ranks, members were firmly linked heart to heart.

In 1786, in the 51st reign year of Cheng-long, the anti-Ching society dared to make several uprisings but was unsuccessful. On November 25 of that year, the Ching troops were called to quell an uprising and to annihilate the members of the Heaven and Earth Society. The Ching soldiers started to burn houses and villages near Dai-toon (Taichung today), about seven miles from Lim Sung-bun's hometown. Innocent people lost their homes, had their farm fields ruined, and were killed for no reason when they were caught by the Ching troops. The soldiers could not really identify the members of the secret society; so, blindly, they struck the people down on the streets or in the fields, like mowing grass or weeds. Everywhere were terrified faces: boys and girls, women and men, young and old, wailing or crying for help, running or crawling to escape. Smoke and fire were everywhere. It was like doomsday.

With this chaotic disorder, the heavens were moving and the earth was shaking. Lim Sung-bun was agitated and determined to end the suffering from such barbarous acts. On November 27, he and his troops raided the Ching forces at night and killed three high-ranking officials and several military leaders. Then Chan-hwa, his home county, was regained. On December 1, he was elected the leader of the alliance, and the people declared allegiance to him. The inaugural ceremony was held in the town of Chan-hwa. The reigning title was *Shun-ten*, Obeying the Mandate of Heaven, and the year became the 1st year of *Shun-ten*. A written summons to all leagues was circulated throughout the island. The people then chopped off their Manchu pigtails and retained their Han topknots, and resumed wearing the Ming (Han) clothing. On December 13, his good friend and loyal comrade Tzun Dai-den regained control of Fong-shan County, which was Tzun's home county.

In March of the following year, Lim Sung-bun, along with Tzun Dai-den and his brother Lim Jung, continued to fight, and regained several towns. Three months later, seeing that the Ching troops were in an inferior position, the emperor Cheng-long sent another 12,000 soldiers and changed the military commanders, discharging the cowardly general and his officers and assigning Fu Kang-an as General of the Army and Hai Lan-tsa as staff officer. More and more soldiers, eventually more than 20,000, were sent across the Taiwan Straits to support, to rescue, and to reinforce the Ching troops. Unfortunately, just at this moment, Lim's troops suffered from internal dissension, which cost them the battle.

Strong, narrow-minded localism has long been regarded as a typical obstacle to national unity in Chinese history. The troops led by Tzun She-shar, whose birthplace was Zwan-chiu, refused to cooperate with the troops led by Tzun Dai-den, whose birthplace was Tsan-chiu. To reduce the tension, Tzun Dai-den suggested changing the troops but Tzun She-shar, who later defected to the Ching government, refused. They both were actually residents of the same county, Fong-shan, in Taiwan. The tangled knot was that their original birthplaces on the mainland were different. Also, the Ching leaders knew how to play on human weaknesses, alienating Tzun Dai-den from Tzun She-shar by spreading rumors.

This strong localism also caused Tzu I-kui of Fokien and his partner Dou Gun-ing of Quantung to lose the battle. Their coalition could not overcome this obstacle, so it was dissolved.

In early December, Lim's troops were totally defeated. Lim Sung-bun had no choice but to retreat into the deep mountains in Poh-li. The Ching troops kept searching and hunting for his body, which was worth 10,000 taels of gold, but had no luck. On January 4, 1788, Lim appeared at his friend Ge Tzin's house and said to him: "Here, I will give you a chance to become wealthy with a high official rank." Then, he stretched out his two wrists in a form of "X" and asked his friend to tie him and take him to the Ching troops.

And this heartless friend really did hand him over to the Ching troops. What kind of friend was Ge Tzin? Even a dog doesn't bite an acquaintance. What did he receive as a reward for selling a friend? It could have been a thousand taels of gold and a high rank. But his guilty conscience would be heavier than all the taels of gold.

Another version judges Ge Tzin's moral character and behavior differently. It is said that Lim Sung-bun himself begged his friend Ge Tzin to tie him and to take him to the Ching troops, because he was tired of running and hiding. Thus, Ge Tzin does not become the scapegoat for Lim Sung-bun's arrest. Lim knew that he surely could not escape from being hunted night and day and having hug the ground. He thought that if he were to be caught sooner or later, he would prefer it to be now to make his body worth someone's fortune. Here you can see an example of his generous and philanthropic nature—even at the end of his days, he wanted to sacrifice his life and make it useful for someone.

On February 5 Tzun Dai-den was defeated in a southern town and taken captive. Because he was badly wounded, the Ching troops did not bother sending him to the Manchu court in Beijing but executed him in the capital of Taiwan by slowly torturing him to death.

Lim Sung-bun, Yen Yen, and the other leaders, including their nine degrees of kindred, were sent to Beijing and also slowly tortured to death. Confiscating property and exterminating the families of the traitors was the rule in China in the old times. The cruel manner of execution was meant not only to punish the traitors but also to warn others of the consequence of rebellion. This warning is well known as a proverbial saying: "To chop up a chicken to teach a monkey." In other words, "Don't act like a monkey and imitate the rebels." (Chicken, fighting cock, is a synonym for troublemaker, and monkey is a copycat.)

Later, Fu Kang-an, the General of the Army, sent a written report to the throne and explained the importance of alleviating the unbalanced Yin–Yang social problem—too many men and not enough women—and suggested that the men coming to Taiwan should be allowed to bring their dependents. The suggestion was immediately approved by the emperor. And from that time on, the Hollos-Hakkas floating logs were seen sailing on white waves with long hair and long gowns in rainbow colors fluttering in the scented wind. This was another benefit of Lim Sung-bun's sacrifice.

Here let me embellish Lim Sung-bun's story with the unresolved riddle of my great-great-great-great-uncles Lim Tung and Lim Zuh, who lived very close to the place where the Lim Sung-bun event occurred. Lim Sung-bun's troops were totally defeated in early December of 1787, the same year in which Zuh died. Was Zuh one of the victims who was blindly mowed down? Or was he one of the volunteers for justice? Or was he one of the members of that secret society? He died when he was only forty-four years old, and his elder brother Tung died three years earlier in 1784, when he was only forty-five years old. Was Tung's death related to Ching's earlier annihilation of the members of the secret society? During the Ching government's blindly crackdowns, an innocent person could be easily killed by accident; was Tung that innocent person? Or was Tung a chicken and Zuh a monkey? I still can find no answer for the riddle, but I would like to assume that they each ate, at different times, an immortal peach and ascended to the Origin of the Peach Blossom, to a utopia. *"Ah-mi-duo-for*! They were really freeing themselves from suffering a mundane existence," to quote a Buddhist saying.

There was a cemetery outside the town of Dai-li-khit, which it is said was once the residence of Lim Sung-bun. After he was sent to Beijing in 1788, his residence was razed. Here I want to tell you that he actually did not die; I mean his **spirit** did not die then. He was transformed into a mango tree, growing up from an urn in the kitchen of the house that was once his own residence. He stood there and laughingly watched the fall of the Ching Dynasty 124 years later; in other words, his spirit outlasted the Ching Dynasty. Thirty-four years later, his spirit as a mango tree saw another foreign regime, the Japanese dynasty, leave the stage in Taiwan and was happy to see the restoration of Taiwan to Han hands in 1945. Ironically, he stood on his own Han land for exactly two dozen years until 1969, but what songs have his fellow Hans of the new breed sung to him? There is no song, no monument, or any other recognition to memorialize his contribution as a martyr to Han's dignity and liberty.

While in high school, a couple of times at the dinner table I heard my uncle Bun-zu, uncle Bun-hiang, and my father, in his early sixties, talking and waving with joy like three old, young boys about having used a long bamboo stick to pick mangos from the fruitful Lim-Sung-bun tree when they were schoolboys. The tree actually benefited the people of the nearby towns and the villages for more than one hundred years. So, you can see again the generous nature of Lim Sung-bun, who never forgot to give away what he had.

How brief is the span of life! Especially the mere thirty years for Lim Sung-bun, who died in the prime of his life. To judge him—merit or demerit—211 years later: Lim Sung-bun was "a martyr of the Ming Dynasty and a rebel of the Ching Dynasty." However, if you compare him with Dr. Sun Yat-sen, who overthrew the Manchu court and founded the Republic of China in 1911, without doubt, Lim Sung-bun was really a martyr of the Hans. He was a man of merit, which righteous act failed to win its rewards. Though unsuccessful, he should be counted as a hero, a hero of no monument or temple, an unsung hero.

Ma-tzo-po, the Goddess of All Trades

On both sides stand her two pacified demon-officials:
the green-faced and green-dressed General Silver and
the red-faced and red-dressed General Gold.

8. The Goddess of All Trades

The path of life is sometimes neither straight nor smooth but often bumpy and rugged. Therefore, when one's spirit is dampened or one suffers a setback, he or she mostly seeks solace from grief through religion or belief. And the power of such spiritual solace is so immeasurable that it sometimes can make a mountain move and a lake dry up. For example, just on the strength of belief in Ma-tzo's divine assistance, the Ching soldiers and the Hans (the Hollos and the Hakkas) overcame their fear of the dangerous black whirlpools and came across the Taiwan Straits in small flatboats that seemed like floating leaves to Taiwan and to other South Pacific islands.

The belief of Ma-tzo, as it is pronounced in Taiwanese, is as popular today as it was a thousand years ago. It is a folk belief and has been widely propagated among the southern coastal provinces. Regrettably, it provides no enlightened doctrine comparable to the philosophical teachings of Confucianism and the nihility-awakening scriptures of Buddhism. Some people say that its occultism actually is derived from the dark side of Taoism, so the belief of Ma-tzo is sorcery and has a blend of Taoism, spiritualism, Buddhism, and a touch of Confucianism. However, some of her advocators insist that Ma-tzo is an incarnation of Kuan-yin, the Buddhist Goddess of Mercy.

Who was Ma-tzo? Why and how did she become the goddess of so many people's hearts? I have combined the information that I learned from the book *The Folk Belief of Ma-tzo*[1] with my own informed resources to introduce you to the Goddess of All Trades.

Ma-tzo, literally, mother ancestress, was born as Lim Mo-neun on Mei-chiu island, Pu-tien, Fokien. Her birthday was on the 23rd day of the 3rd moon in 960 in the first year of the reign of Jien-long of the Northern Sung Dynasty. It is said that a glaring red ray came from the northwest and shone into her mother's chamber when she was in labor. During her birth the air was full of fragrance. Until a full month after birth, the baby never cried once, so her father

---

1. *The Folk Belief of Ma-tzo* is written in Chinese by Lu-lu Lee.

Lim Guan, a civil officer, named his sixth daughter Mo-neun, quiet girl.

At the age of eight, she received family tutoring, and quickly was able to read and comprehend well many books. At the age of ten, she dreamed of being a Buddha and chanted the Buddhist scriptures day and night. One day during her teens, when she was playing outside of her house, she met a very old and shabbily dressed pauper. Kindheartedly, she gave him some tea and some silver coins. In return, the pauper gave her a tiny wooden man, and said solemnly, "If you encounter any trouble, light incense and let the smoke rings encircle this wooden man. Then you will get a message telling you what to do."

Time passed. One day when her mother was very sick, she remembered what the old pauper had told her. She lit incense and hurriedly tried to smoke out the secret knowledge. In a flash, a line of text was displayed behind the wooden man. It said, "Look for Xuan-tong[2] in South Mountain." Alone, she went far and deep to South Mountain, where she came upon a stone statue that looked like the old pauper. She knelt down before him and begged. The Taoist, the pauper, was moved by her sincerity and revealed his true identity. Immediately he gave her the cure, the wonder drug, that saved her mother's life. She

2. A Taoist, a spiritualist, or a metaphysicist who understands the profound and mysterious truth.

later learned from him the occult sciences, including divination, medicine, astrology, and physiognomy.

There is another version of the story about how Ma-tzo became a sorceress. One day at age sixteen, she was playing in the countryside with her sisters and other girls. Happily, they found a well in which the water was as clear as a mirror. The girls sniffed the old well and tried to find something in it, but saw only their own curious, beautiful faces. As soon as they walked away from the well, a divine man emerged with a copper *fu*, a talisman, in his hands. The other girls were frightened and ran away, but Ma-tzo knelt down before the man and accepted the copper *fu*. The godlike man then rose straight up and disappeared in a rainbow of clouds. After receiving the copper *fu*, Ma-tzo engrossed herself in studying the science of *fu*. Later, she mastered the sorcery of *fu* and practiced its charm in many ways, including subduing demons, exorcising evil spirits, forecasting natural phenomena, guiding sailors, caring for the sick, predicting one's lot and correcting one's destiny. Obviously, she possessed profound and marvelous abilities and was very resourceful.

Ma-tzo died on the 9th day of the 9th moon in 987, in the fourth year of the reign of Yung-hsi, after living only twenty-seven years. (The Chinese count it as twenty-eight years; a 280-day-old fetus is counted as one year old since its heart beats already before it is born.) After her death, people deified her. Instead of saying that she passed away, they said she ascended to heaven and became an immortal.

On the day she ascended, she first told her family that she was going to a faraway place and asked her sisters not to come with her. Then she ferried across the sea to Mei-chiu Island and climbed up to the peak of Mount Mei, which stood in a mist of heavy clouds. During her ascent, crisp melodies like cracking bamboo or splitting silk from heaven echoed through the glens. Her long sleeves flapped like white bird-wings on a bright day. She rose up and up, higher and higher until she reached a rainbow of clouds that closed around her. Everyone was amazed to see such an unbelievable scene and submitted to her divine being.

Today, the 9th day of the lunar 9th month is called "Mountain Climbing Day," which must be associated with this legend; people celebrate this day by taking mountain hikes or just long hikes. Amusingly, the Chinese name the 9th month of the year the Xuan-yueh, or the Taoist moon.

Hmm. . . , just a thought: my mother died on the 9th day of the 9th moon, too. Does it mean something about her death? If she had ascended to heaven and become a goddess on that specific day like Ma-tzo, she should have been the Chinese Goddess of Flora or Pomona, because she had planted a garden of flowers and fruit trees and loved and cared about them during her short lifetime.

Ma-tzo was a kind-hearted woman when she was living, and she was deified after her death. As the years rolled on, she became the Goddess of All Trades. As the Goddess of the Sea, she was either flying on a straw mat or riding on an iron horse while saving drowning people, and she was directing the sails to ensure a safe voyage. As the Goddess of Rain and Wind, she was dancing with her long, fan-like sleeves to pray for rain when people suffered from seasons of drought, and she was fanning the four winds to chase away the clouds when people were afflicted with overcast days. As the Goddess of Birth and Upbringing, she was asked for help in granting a son or many sons to continue the family line, and parents sought assistance from her magic *fu* or herbs to expel evil spirits and illness in raising decent and healthy children. As the Goddess of Wars, she was cast by the ruling class during many dynasties as a protector of wars, and with her divine help, many glories were won. The key of this psywar (psychological warfare), of course, was to increase the morale of the soldiers and to scare away the enemies. The Ching government also practiced this trick during the crackdowns of Tzu I-kui and Lim Sung-bun. To this end, each emperor gave her many different titles to promote her divine power in wars, ending with Empress of Heaven.

To conclude Ma-tzo's life and her exploits, I wouldn't want to say she was a sorceress. Some descriptions of what she did during her short lifetime are overpainting and exaggerating. I would rather like to compare her with today's Cheng-yen Dharma Master, the founder of Tzu-chi Foundation. Ma-tzo's good deeds of high glory—helping the poor and needy, the sick, and the luckless—were done out of pure benevolence as Cheng-yen Dharma Master does in Taiwan and worldwide. Ma-tzo's accomplishment through her compassion has touched the hearts of people in the old days and so today, too.

Today there are about 10 million Ma-tzo worshippers, and her spirit is shared among 4,000 cloned Ma-tzo statues in about 20 countries, according to a newspaper report in spring 1998. However, there is no Ma-tzo temple to be found in Parasol Tree Village. That doesn't mean that the villagers do not worship her; on the contrary, a big yearly festival in her honor has been held in this small village for quite a long time. The following is an account of the origin of the festival, as told by the old-timers.

Some time ago, the rice fields in the area encompassing Parasol Tree Village and seventeen other villages suffered from a long-standing blight, and the heartsick farmers could find no method to prevent or to control it. Everyone hated to see fields and fields of green rice shoots withered and yellow. One day someone suggested that they ask help from the mighty Ma-tzo-po.[3] Others echoed this uncertain suggestion. A statue of the goddess was borrowed from Han-keh, the only village with a Ma-tzo temple, to be asked to perform a miracle. On the day of the borrowing, Ma-tzo was carried in a palanquin and paraded around the rice fields of one village. In the next few days, a strange thing happened. Wherever she had passed by, the withered and yellowish rice shoots stood straight and strong and green.

The story of this miracle spread quickly mouth-to-mouth, and the other villagers argued about who would be next to receive her blessing. To satisfy all eighteen villages, a one-day schedule for each was set up, calling this day the "Ma-tzo Procession Day." It started on the first day of the 3rd moon in the village of Eh-po-tzu, with Parasol Tree Village being allotted the eighth day, and ended on the 20th day back in her home village of Han-keh, in time for her birthday on the 23rd day. Since that time, the Ma-tzo Procession Day has become a traditional yearly festival in Parasol Tree Village and seventeen other villages.

This festival is busy with activities. On the procession day, Ma-tzo is always greeted with great pomp and ceremony. She is glamorously dressed in sparkling gold and glittering red and richly bejeweled. (My sister Shiu-bue used to make

3. "Po" is a term of respect for an old lady. Ma-tzo-po is commonly called by the people in Taiwan.

fun of someone who was overdressed by saying "She looks like Ma-tzo-po today.") A variety of colorful, festive flags and streamers lead the noisy, festive procession. Ma-tzo sits in a wood-trimmed glass box in a gaily decorated palanquin, carried by a team of ten strong men. On both sides stand her two subdued and pacified demon-officials: the green-faced and green-dressed General Silver, whose eyes see targets as far as a thousand miles away, and the red-faced and red-dressed General Gold, whose ears hear sounds as smooth as a sail with favorable winds. Stinking and deafening firecrackers, ear-splitting gongs, drums, cymbals, flutes, pipes, and chimes fill the air. The solemn-faced worshippers hold smoke-spiraling incense sticks and follow like human dragons as the procession parades through the main streets and wider lanes.

On the table of each house the villagers offer sacrifices to worship her, including tea, fruits, fragrant flowers, and, not least, a set of a woman's make-up items: a mirror, a comb, a lipstick, and a box of face powder, too. After the street parade is over, Ma-tzo is placed in a temporary tent temple to take a rest and also to enjoy what the village offers to entertain her, either a melancholy Taiwanese opera or a delightful puppet show.

In the meantime, every family is busy preparing foods in the kitchen and greeting known or unknown guests in the living room for a treat of lunch or dinner. Frequently, the dining tables are set in the courtyard or outside of the house; usually, two to three tables are needed for fifteen to twenty guests at meal time. There are also some people who simply follow the Ma-tzo procession through all the eighteen villages and dine at the tables with no acquaintance, sponging big, free meals for eighteen days.

To accommodate pilgrims and sightseers at the Ma-tzo Temple in Mei-chiu, plans have been drawn to renew the existing structure and add more beautiful and splendid buildings. A ground-breaking ceremony was held in the spring of 1998. The 30-million-dollar cost of the construction, focused on a style resembling that of an imperial palace, will be paid by the generous donations of her faithful worshippers on both sides of the sea, Taiwan and the mainland.

When the so-called original Ma-tzo of Mei-chiu came to visit her spiritually subdivided or shared temples in Taiwan in 1997, there was much excitement. Ma-tzo, acting as ambassador, brought cultural and political amity between two sides of nations since the mainland became Communist in 1949. Her visit made her Taiwanese worshippers quite infatuated with her. With all her fascinating magic powers, Ma-tzo could play a new role as a peacemaker between the two lands in the coming century.

Lim-Nan Kuan-neun (1667 - 1777)   Lim Guan-jiang (1667- 1729)

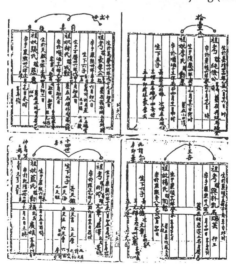

Tables 3, 4, and 5, written in hair pencil by family members
in different generations, are our own family tree, which
started from around 600 B. C..

9. A Tree of 3,133 Rings

There is no sound, no color, and no smell as it passes you by,
and you neither can see it nor can feel it as you let it go by.

It is neither a mist of flowers nor a fog of stars.

It comes when the nightingale lulls you at night,
and it goes when the morning dove arouses you at dawn.

When it comes, it is as transient as a spring dream,
and when it goes, it is as traceless as the autumn breeze.

And in just a wink, you see a wrinkled face with
a pepper-and-salt head in the morning mirror.

*T*empus fugit, time flies. The Yin-Yang birds weave wrinkles on one's face night by night and day after day: the warp is crossed by the woof. Time stops for no one: it has no compassion; it never waits for you; it never glances back at you but hurries to chase and glorify the contemporary *you*. A long and ancient passage of three thousand years is seemingly not so far to reach on lines which are just a few dozen pages long, since a life after all is just a piece of name left—its immortal soul rises up to the Celestial City and waits for the right time to be reincarnated, and its perishable flesh is like falling petals that return to mother earth.

A tree has its root, and a stream has its source. One has to know where one comes from. Here, I present to you the 3,133-rings of my family tree. The tree starts with Pi Kan, Father of the Lims; it is about 105 generations or slightly more, and comprises five tables. The first two tables are retrieved from another Lim branch; unexpectedly, three generations 19th, 20th, and 21st in Table 2 are found to be the generations 14th, 15th, and 16th in Table 3. Tables 3, 4, and 5, written in hair pencil by family members in different generations, are our own family tree, which is well kept in the clan temple. My eldest brother Deng-piao accepts and embraces Tables 1 and 2 in the clan genealogy, since they look as if they were related once upon a time. Although skipped lineages are suspected, I thought it is still interesting and worth presenting.

In order to reduce the page count, siblings are omitted. The number of the sons and the order of the siblings are given in the column **Parent/Children** and are showed as **Parent (number of the sons)** and --> *Children, (the order of the siblings)*, respectively. The ancient titles or ranks in the column **Information** may not be completely accurate after translation. In fact, because each dynasty has its own ranking system, it is very hard to trace back and to name them accurately.

A glance at the evolutionary changes in Chinese history is provided in the tables for your reference. Some of the following Chinese history are based on *The Vocabulary of Chinese History*, written by Yen Tai-bei and published in 1984, and some of them are my own research.

TABLE 1. The Inception of the Lim Family

Line-age	Parent/Children	Dynasty/ (Emperor)	Year	Information
Prince Tarng overthrew the tyrant Jye of the first dynasty Hsia (2205 B.C. - 1766 B.C.) and established the second dynasty Shang (1766 B.C. - 1122 B.C.) with its capital in Haur (in Honan today).				
Pan-kgung, the 20th emperor, not only moved the capital to Yin after five different changes to avoid floods but also changed the dynastic title to Yin in 1401 B.C. Thus, the dynasty is also known as Yin-Shang. Later, Emperor Wu-yee, the 28th emperor, changed it to Chaokge. It lasted 644 years with 31 emperors.				
Pi Kan was the uncle and the vice premier (later became the premier as the premier resigned) of Emperor Zoh, the 31st emperor of the Yin Dynasty, who was a tyrant and killed Pi Kan in 1123 B.C..				
Ji Hwa, the second son of Ji Chang, one of the four feudal lords of Emperor Zoh, overturned the Yin Dynasty in 1122 B.C. and became the first emperor, Emperor Wu, of the Chou Dynasty (1122 B.C - 256 B.C.) with its capital in Haw (in Shensi today). The dynasty lasted 866 years with 37 emperors.				
In 1120 B.C. Emperor Wu conferred an hereditary title "The Minister of Poh-lin, *Chin Da Fu*" along with the feudal estates in Poh-lin upon Pi Kan's posthumous son, Kien, and bestowed the family name "Lim." Kien became Lim Kien, and he was the inceptor of Lim. Pi Kan is thus regarded as father of the Lims.				
0	**Pi Kan (2)** --> *Lim Kien (2nd)*	Yin/(Di-yee and Zoh)	1135 B.C.	The vice premier; then the premier.

TABLE 1. **The Inception of the Lim Family (continued)**

Line-age	Parent/Children	Dynasty/ (Emperor)	Year	Information
The Chou Dynasty split into West Chou and East Chou. From the first emperor Emperor Wu in 1122 B.C. to the 12th emperor Emperor Yoh in 770 B.C., who was killed by the western barbarians, the dynasty was named as West Chou because of its capital in Haw (Western).				
1	**Kien (2)** --> *Tsuo (2nd)*	West Chou/ (Wu)	1120 B.C.	The minister of Poh-lin.
2	**Tsuo (3)** --> *Zhen (2nd)*		1115 B.C. - 1091 B.C.	The minister of war.
3	**Zhen (4)** --> *Jian (3rd)*			
4	**Jian (4)** --> *Shiang (4th)*			
5	**Shiang (3)** --> *Chin (3rd)*	(Chiao)	1052 B.C.	A minister.
6	**Chin (1)** --> *Shyuan (1st)*			
7	**Shyuan (1)** --> *Fong (1st)*	(Mou)	1001 B.C.	A minister.
8	**Fong (1)** --> *Tang (1st)*	(Kong)	946 B.C.	An official.
9	**Tang (1)** --> *Yih (1st)*			
10	**Yih (5)** --> *Kai (4th)*	(Li)	878 B.C.	An official.
11	**Kai (1)** --> *Chang (1st)*			
12	**Chang (2)** --> *Tsai (1st)*	(Yao)	781 B.C.	An official.

TABLE 1. The Inception of the Lim Family (continued)

Line-age	Parent/Children	Dynasty/ (Emperor)	Year	Information
To avoid the invasion of the western tribe, Emperor Ping, the 13th emperor of the Chou Dynasty, moved the capital from Haw (Western) to Loyang (Eastern) in 770 B.C. From then until Emperor Naan, who surrendered in 256 B.C. to the ruler of the dynasty's feudal state Chin, it was named East Chou. It lasted 515 years with 25 emperors.				
13	**Tsai (2)** --> *Zhen (1st)*	East Chou/ (Ping)	770 B.C.	The minister of war, who led six army of army and followed Emperor Ping to the new capital, Loyang.
After moving to Loyang, all the feudal states started to contend for power, which resulted in the disintegration and collapse of the feudal system. This was the Epoch of Spring and Autumn (772 B.C. - 403 B.C.), which included the following 14 states: Chin, Tzen, Tzin, Tzao, Sung, Chi, Cheng, Wu, Yue, Tzu, Tsai, Lu, Wei, Yen.				
14	**Zhen (1)** --> *Tsin*			
15	**Tsin (1)** --> *Huei*	(Shi)	681 B.C.	An official.
16	**Huei (2)** --> *Tsuey (1st)*	(Huei)	676 B.C.	An outstanding person in virtuous and learning.
17	**Tsuey (7)** --> *Fu (4th)*			
18	**Fu (1)** --> *Bao*			
19	**Bao (1)** --> *Fung*	(Ching)	618 B.C.	A military vice general.
20	**Fung (1)** --> *Piao*	(Ding)	606 B.C.	A court official.
21	**Piao (2)** --> *Shen (2nd)*	(Jean)	585 B.C.	A military general.

TABLE 1. The Inception of the Lim Family (continued)

Line-age	Parent/Children	Dynasty/ (Emperor)	Year	Information
China's first sage, Confucius, was born in 551 B.C. in Chue-fu, Shangtung Province, in the state of Lu.				
22	**Shen (1)** --> *Huan*			
23	**Huan (1)** --> *Tung*	(Jing)	519 B.C.	A minister.
Lim Huan adopted Confucius' alias "Tzi Chio" as his own and regarded himself as Confucius' disciple and worshipper. Posthumously, he was awarded the title "The Count of West River" by Emperor Xuan -tzong (713 A.D.-755 A.D.) of the Tang Dynasty and the title "The Marquis of Chang Shan" by Emperor Kao-tzong of the Sung Dynasty (1127-1162).				
24	**Tung (1)** --> *Bu-neou*	(Jing)		A county magistrate.
25	**Bu-neou (1)** --> *Fuu*	Lu/ (Ai-kung)	484 B.C.	A high official who died for his country as a martyr.
26	**Fuu (2)** --> *Shiow (1st)*	East Chou/ (Yuan)	475 B.C.	The magistrate of Ching-chou.
27	**Shiow (3)** --> *Xin (2nd)*			
The Epoch of Warring States (403 B.C. - 221 B.C.), when the 14 states of the Epoch of Spring and Autumn merged into seven states (Chin, Tzu, Chi, Hang, Chao, Wei, Yen). The seven states contended for hegemony. Chin used her famous strategem—uniting the distant states and attacking the neighboring ones—to become the unchallenged ruler of the empire under Chin Shih-huang, the Emperor of Beginning, or the First Emperor of China, the name he called himself. He united China.				
28	**Xin (1)** --> *Rung*	(Ceng-leh)	425 B.C.	A magistrate.

TABLE 1. **The Inception of the Lim Family (continued)**

Line-age	Parent/Children	Dynasty/ (Emperor)	Year	Information
29	**Rung (3)** --> *Shi-yuan (1st)*	(An)	401 B.C.	A military vice general.
30	**Shi-yuan (1)** --> *Bor*	(Shean)	368 B.C.	The minister of public affairs.
31	**Bao (1)** --> *Sean*	(Shean)	368 B.C.	The minister of public affairs.
32	**Sean (1)** --> *Wei*	(Shen-jing)	320 B.C.	The minister of war.
33	**Wei (3)** --> *Fung (1st)*	(Nean)	314 B.C.	A minister.
34	**Fung (1)** --> *Bao-kgee*	Chin/ (Zao-shiang)	288 B.C.	A military official in charge of archery.
35	**Bao-kgee (1)** --> *Yee*	(Hsiao-wen)		A scholar of profound learning.
36	**Yee (3)** --> *Wei (2nd)*	(Zuang-shiang)	249 B.C.	An imperial chief teacher.
37	**Wei (2)** --> *Shaur (1st)*	Chin/(Shih-huang,)	246 B.C.	A military vice general in administration.
38	**Shaur (1)** --> *Zuan*	(Shih-huang)	224 B.C.	The magistrate of Yu-lin.

Liu Pang destroyed Chin and Tzu, consolidated the states, and formed the Han Dynasty with its capital in Chang-an in 206 B.C. The dynasty later divided into Former (Western) Han (206 B.C. - 23 A.D.) and Latter (Eastern) Han (25 A.D. - 220 A.D.) with its capital in Loyang.

The Former (Western) Han Dynasty was usurped in 9 A.D. by Wang Mang, the prime minister, who had introduced many reforms. The seizure of power caused many deaths among the population.

| 39 | **Zuan (1)**
 --> *Chyu* | Former Han/ (Hwei) | 194 B.C. | The magistrate of Chung-shan. |

TABLE 1. The Inception of the Lim Family (continued)

Line-age	Parent/Children	Dynasty/ (Emperor)	Year	Information
40	**Chyu (5)** --> *Pei (2nd)*	(Hwei)	194 B.C.	A military commander.
41	**Pei (1)** --> *Kgaw*	(Wen)	179 B.C.	A minister in public affairs.
42	**Kgaw (1)** --> *Shuh*	(Wen)	179 B.C.	A marquis of Kgau-dien.
43	**Shuh (1)** --> *Liang*	(Jiing)	156 B.C.	One (the last) of the nine ministers.
44	**Liang (2)** --> *Kung (1st)*	(Wu)	139 B.C.	A lieutenant general.
45	**Kung (2)** --> *Tze (1st)*	(Wu)	104 B.C.	A prefecture censor.
46	**Tze (1)** --> *Ping*	(Zao)	86 B.C.	Emperor Xuan conferred the title of Pacifying General.
47	**Ping (1)** --> *Kgau*	(Xuan)	72 B.C.	A general in charge of the western territory.
48	**Kgau (5)** --> *Mia (2nd)*	(Yuan)	48 B.C.	A military general; the governor of Jian-chou.
49	**Mia (2)** --> *Chio (2nd)*	(Tzen)	32 B.C.	The magistrate of Ping-yuan.
50	**Chio (1)** --> *Fung*	Latter Han/ (Shang)	106 A.D.	The minister of defense.
51	**Fung (1)** --> *Lung*	(Huan)	167 A.D.	The governor of Chin-chou.
52	**Lung (1)** --> *Tzi*	(Hsien)	191	An official in charge of court secretarial duties.

TABLE 1. The Inception of the Lim Family (continued)

Lineage	Parent/Children	Dynasty/ (Emperor)	Year	Information
Tung Tso, a prime minister at the end of the Latter Han Dynasty, gave a false report to the emperor, pointing out that the Lims were too powerful and threatening; therefore, 747 high ranking officials of the Lims were demoted and sent in exile to the fields. Tung Tso was executed in the year 192 because of this false report.				
53	**Tzi (1)** --> *Hu*	(Hsien)	219	A general in charge of the archery troops.
After the Han Dynasty, the Chinese world was sliced into the so-called Three Kingdoms:				

Kingdom	Capital	Emperor	Territory
Wei (220 - 264)	Loyang	Tsao Tsao	The Yellow River area.
Shu (221 - 263)	Cherng-doo	Liu Pei	Pa-Shu, two ancient states in Szechwan.
Wu (222 - 277)	Chien-yeh	Sun Chyuan	The Jiang-su area, the lower reaches of the Yangtze River.

The major battle at the Red Cliff was an exciting historical episode in this epoch. *The Romance of theThree Kingdoms* by Lo Kuan-chung of the Yuan Dynasty (1279 - 1367 A.D.) is the most popular novel mixing history and fiction about the Epoch of the Three Kingdoms.

Lineage	Parent/Children	Dynasty/ (Emperor)	Year	Information
54	**Hu (3)** --> *Tang (2nd)*	The Three Kingdoms/ (Wei -Wen)	220	The magistrate of Tung-lei and Cheng-liu.
55	**Tang (2)** --> *Yu (2nd)*	(Wei - Ming)	227	An official in charge of court secretarial duties.
56	**Yu (1)** --> *Tao Ku*	(Wei - Ming)	229	The magistrate of Ho-tung and Ho-nan.
57	**Tao Ku (1)** --> *Kwan*	(Wei - Chi)	240	A court historiographer.

TABLE 1. The Inception of the Lim Family (continued)

Line-age	Parent/Children	Dynasty/ (Emperor)	Year	Information
58	**Kwan (1)** --> *Yu*	(Wei - Cheng-liu)	260	The governor of Chin-chou.
	Suu-Ma Yen was the founding emperor, Emperor Wu, of the Tsin Dynasty (265 - 420). Until Emperor Miin was kidnapped, the dynasty had its capital in Loyang and was known as the Western Tsin Dynasty (265 - 316). Zwei, the ruler of Liang-ya (Shantung today) and one of the imperial clansman, took the throne and became Emperor Yen of the Eastern Tsin Dynasty (317 - 419). He moved southward and had his capital in Chien-kan. (Superstitiously, he renamed Chien-yeh as Chien-kan, good health, Nan-jing today). Chien-yeh was east of Loyang, so the dynasty was called the Eastern Tsin.			
59	**Yu (5)** --> *Fung Shiun* *(2nd)*	The West Tsin/(Wu)	266	A courtier and a military general in jurisdiction.
60	**Fung Shiun (1)** --> *Hsien*	(Wu)	271	The magistrate of Poh-lin.
61	**Hsien (2)** --> *Li (2nd)*	(Wu)	280	The magistrate of Poh-lin and Shan-yan.

TABLE 1. The Inception of the Lim Family (continued)

Line-age	Parent/Children	Dynasty/ (Emperor)	Year	Information
The Big Migration: In 304 the five northern barbarian tribes, including Hun, Tungusic, Jye, Di, and Jiang, invaded and occupied the Central Plain along the Yellow River. The Hans ran for their lives to the south. It was such a catastrophe that a family of ten, six would be separated or even killed. The parents and their children never met again in life and longed to see each other, but could only see in dreams. The whole nation wailed in pain.				
After the Western Tsin founder Emperor Wu died, the dynasty fell into disorder—The Upheaval of the Eight Princes. Eight feudal rulers fought each other for power. Liu Yeng of Hun first rose and established his state, the Former Chao, then the other fifteen states as follows: Chen Han (Di), the Latter Chao (Jye), the Former Liang (Han), the Former Yen (Tungusic), the Former Chin (Di), the Latter Yen (Tungusic), the Latter Chin (Jiang), the Western Chin (Tungusic), the Latter Liang (Di), the Southern Liang (Tungusic), the Northern Liang (Hun), the Southern Yen (Tungusic), the Western Liang (Han), Hsia (Hun), and the Northern Yen (Han).				
62	**Li (1)** --> *Ing*	The Five Barbarian Tribes and the Sixteen States/ (Tsin -Whi)	307	The imperial teacher for princes.
63	**Ing (2)** --> *Luu (2nd)*	(Tsin Min)	315	A military official of Hsu-chou.
In 317, the capital Loyang was taken over by the barbarians. Lim Ing followed Emperor Yuan, moving from north to south; literally, he brought the Lim seeds to the south and scattered them in Chiang-tso, Jiang-su today.				

TABLE 1. The Inception of the Lim Family (continued)

Line-age	Parent/Children	Dynasty/ (Emperor)	Year	Information
64	**Luu (2)** --> *Jiing (1st)*	(Yuan)	317	The marquis of Tsin-an.

In 325, Lim Luu, the second son of Lim Ing, followed Emperor Yuan moving farther south to Fokien. Thus, Lim Luu became the founder of the Fokien chapter.

TABLE 2. The Fokien Founding Chapter

Line-age	Parent/Children	Dynasty/ (Emperor)	Year	Information
1	**Luu (2)** --> *Jiing (1st)*	The Five Barbarian Tribes and the Sixteen States/(East Tsin - Ming)	325	Lim Luu 289 - 356. Wife: Kong 293 - 363. The marquis of Tsin-An was the last of several titles.
2	**Jiing (2)** --> *Huan (1st)*	(East Tsin - Chen)	330	The marquis of Nan-pin. Wives: Su-ma and Huang.
3	**Huan (5)** --> *Kger (3rd)*	(East Tsin - Mou)	355	The marquis of Nan-pin. Wife: Huang.
4	**Kger (5)** --> *Ching-tzi (5th)*	(East Tsin - Shiao-wu)	373	A minister in the imperial court.
5	**Ching-tzi (6)** --> *Suei-tzi (4th)*	(East Tsin - Shiao-wu)	387	1. A heroic general. 2. The magistrate of Chen-yan.

TABLE 2. The Fokien Founding Chapter (continued)

Lineage	Parent/Children	Dynasty/(Emperor)	Year	Information
After the Eastern Tsin, China was divided into the Han-ruled south and the barbarian north, which was the Epoch of North and South (420 - 589 A.D.). The establishment of this North and South confrontation is shown below:				

E = East, F = Former, L = Latter, N = North, W = West, S = South

6	Suei-tzi (8) --> Dun-ming (8th)	The North and South Epoch/(Sung)	423	The magistrate of Nan-hai.
7	Dun-ming (7) --> Yu-jen (7th)	(Sung - Hsiao-wu)	457	An impeachment official.
8	Yu-jen (3) --> Yuan-tzu (3rd)	(Sung - Ming)	465	A high official. Wife: Cheng.
9	Yuan-tzu (3) --> Maw (2nd)	(Liang - Wu Di)	483	The magistrate of Jen-an.

TABLE 2. The Fokien Founding Chapter (continued)

Line-age	Parent/Children	Dynasty/(Emperor)	Year	Information
Yang Kien seized the Northern Chou state, defeated the Chen state, and consolidated the Northern and Southern states. He formed the Sui Dynasty in the year 581 and ended 150 years (439 - 589) of strife. He became the first emperor, Emperor Wen (541-604), of the Sui Dynasty.				

Sung, Chi, Liang, Chen, and the Northern Chi were the Hans; the Northern Wei and the Northern Chou were the Tungusics, who lived in Manchuria and eastern Mongolia from 2nd to 7th century A.D.. Emperor Hsiao-wen of the Northern Wei adopted the Han culture and demanded that everyone change the Tungusic name to the Han name. He changed his family name from Toba to Yuen.

The development of the epoch is shown below:

[The South Dynasty] Sung — Chi — Liang — Chen ——————————— Sui

[The North Dynasty] North Wei ⟨ East Wei — North Chi ⟩ North Chou

West Wei — North Chou ⟩

10	**Maw (1)** --> *Hsiao-bao*	Sui/(Wen)	583	The premier. Wife: Natzduh (She could be a Tungus.)
11	**Hsiao-bao (3)** --> *Wen-chi (3rd)*	(Wen)	586	The magistrate of Honan; the governor of Chen-chou. Wife: Wang.
12	**Wen-chi (5)** --> *Kou-du (4th)*	Sui		The magistrate of Lo-chou; An imperial censor. Wife: Chang.
13	**Kou-du (3)** --> *Shyen-tai (3rd)*	Sui		A military staff officer. Wives: Cheng and Wu.

TABLE 2. The Fokien Founding Chapter (continued)

Line-age	Parent/Children	Dynasty/ (Emperor)	Year	Information
The last Sui emperor abdicated the throne to Lee Yen, who became Emperor Kao-tzu and changed the dynasty to Tang; the capital remained in Chang-an. In 684, Empress Wu, famous for her lasciviousness, usurped the throne from the fourth emperor and ruled for twenty years. She changed the dynastic title to Chou in 690, but Emperor Chung-tzong resumed the throne in 707. The Tang Dynasty lasted 290 years (618 - 907) with 20 rulers.				
14	**Shyen-tai (5)** --> *Won-long (1st)*	Tang/ (Empress Wu)	689	The governor of Yin-chou. Wife: Wu.
15	**Won-long (3)** --> *Chang (3rd)*	Tang/ (Xuan-tzong)	720	The magistrate of Rau-chou, then of Kau-ping.
16	**Chang (1)** --> *Ping*			A scholar lived in seclusion; then became a high official. Wife: Sung.
17	**Ping (1)** --> *Dien-yu*			A prefecture magistrate.
18	**Dien-yu (3)** --> *Ho-hsiao (2nd)*			Wife: Tsai.
The following three generations, 19, 20, and 21 are the same generations, 14, 15, 16 in Table 3, which starts our family genealogy, circa A.D. 600 in the Tang Dynasty.				
19	**Ho-hsiao (1)** --> *Yuan*			See the lineage 14 **Hsiao** in Table 3. **Ho-hsiao** and **Hsiao** should be the same person.

TABLE 2. The Fokien Founding Chapter (continued)

Line-age	Parent/Children	Dynasty/(Emperor)	Year	Information
20	**Yuan (5)** --> *Chien-yi-long* --> *Chien-zi-long* --> *Chien-san-long* --> *Chien-si-long* *(4th)* --> *Chien-go-long*			See Table 3, Lineage 15.
21	**Chien-si-long (2)** --> *Rong-tzun (1st)*			

TABLE 3. The Fokien Chapter I

Line-age	Parent/Children	Dynasty/(Emperor)	Year	Information
1	**Chen-yuan (9)** --> *Tzen-kuei (1st)*	Tang/(Tai-tzong and Kao-tzong)	600-700s	A high official. Wives: Chen, Yin.
	Lim Chen-yuan was a high official in 627-649, promoted in 669 after assisting Chen Yuen-kwan, the Saint of Developing Tsan-chou, and ennobled posthumously as the General in Defense by Emperor Kao-tzong of the Sung Dynasty (1150). Both of his wives were granted an honorable title.			
2	**Tzen-kuei (1)** --> *Tzin*			
3	**Tzin (1)** --> *Shyan*	Tang/(Hsien-tzong)	807	A well-learned man; appointed an official in charge of salt and iron, later joined the military.
4	**Shyan (2)** --> *Chao (2nd)*			
5	**Chao (1)** --> Dai-leh			

TABLE 3. The Fokien Chapter I (continued)

Line-age	Parent/ Children	Dynasty/ (Emperor)	Year	Information
6	**Dai-leh (3)** --> *Shi-tze (1st)*			
7	**Shi-tze (1)** --> *Kwang*			

During the reign of Emperor Hsi-tzong, the cruel Huang Chao led a ten-year rebellion (874 - 884) that shook the base of the Tang Dynasty. Tang fell in 907. Between the Tang Dynasty and the Sung Dynasty, there was the Epoch of the Five Dynasties: The posterior Liang Dynasty (16 years), the Posterior Tang Dynasty (13 years), the Posterior Tsin Dynasty (11 years), the Posterior Han Dynasty (4 years), and the Posterior Chou Dynasty (9 years), a total of 53 years.

Chao Kuang-yin, who defeated the Posterior Chou in 960, became Emperor Tai-tzu and named the dynasty Sung.

Until 1126, when Emperor Hwei-tzong and Emperor Chin-tzong were kidnapped by the Jins, historians called this dynasty the Northern Sung Dynasty, which lasted 167 years (960 - 1126) with 9 emperors. The Jins were the Nuechen, or the Jurchens, ancestors of the Manchus.

The tenth emperor, Emperor Kao-tzong, moved southward to Ling-an. The historians called his dynasty the Southern Sung, which lasted 153 years (1127 - 1279) with 9 emperors. The Sung Dynasty lasted 320 years with 18 emperors.

Line-age	Parent/ Children	Dynasty/ (Emperor)	Year	Information
8	**Kwang (7)** --> *Yi (3rd)*	Sung/ (Tai-tzu)	960	A teacher of Confucian subjects.

Ma-tzo, The Goddess of All Trades, was born in the year 960.

Line-age	Parent/ Children	Dynasty/ (Emperor)	Year	Information
9	**Yi (1)** --> *Yee*			
10	**Yee (1)** --> *Wan*			
11	**Wan (1)** --> *Chi-jen*			

TABLE 3. The Fokien Chapter I (continued)

Line-age	Parent/ Children	Dynasty/ (Emperor)	Year	Information
12	**Chi-jen (2)** --> *Bor (1st)*			
13	**Bor (2)** --> *Hsiao (1st)*	(Kao-tzong)	1150	
	The Khitan Tartars and the Nuechens invaded China and established their own dynasties, the Liao Dynasty (916-1168) and the Jin Dynasty (1115-1234), respectively.			
14	**Hsiao (1)** --> *Yuan*	(Ning-tzong)	1208 - 1224	He should be **Ho-hsiao**. See the lineage 19 in Table 2. A high military official. He wielded both pen and sword. Wife: Wu.
15	**Yuan (5)** --> *Chien-yi-long* --> *Chien-zi-long* --> *Chien-san-long* --> *Chien-si-long* *(4th)* --> *Chien-go-long*			He inherited the rank and the title. Wife: Lee passed away after delivering a girl; he then married Su-maWu.
16	**Chien-si-long (2)** --> *Rong-tzun (1st)*	Sung/ (Li-tzong) - Yuan/ (Chen-tzong)	1225 - 1299	The Lim branch titled "Lane Head," a place name where he lived, was originated by him and started from his lineage.

TABLE 4. **The Fokien Chapter II**

Line-age	Parent/ Children	Dynasty/ (Emperor)	Year	Information
1	Chien-si-long (2) --> *Rong-tzun (1st)*	Sung/ (Li-tzong) - Yuan/ (Chen-tzong)	1225 - 1299	Wife: Wu.
2	Rong-tzun (3) --> *Tzung-chen (1st)*			
3	Tsung-chen (2) --> *Dau-sheh (1st)*			
4	Dau-sheh (3) --> *Jen-shian (1st)*			
5	Jen-shian (2) --> *Tzung-yuan (2nd)*	Yuan/ (Shun-di) - Ming/ (Tai-tzu)	1335 - 1418	See below for details.

Lim Jen-shian, led his troops against the Mongols and achieved a great deal of merit. But owing to inferior strength, he and his brother resigned and went back home. He then helped the Buddhist master built a grand temple and administered its business. Soon, he established a school for the public, set up rules warning his descendants against indulging in gambling and the pursuit of pleasure.

Chu Yuan-chang, a Han Chinese peasant and once a Buddhist monk, conquered all others, chased out the Mongols, and became Emperor Tai-tzu of the Ming Dynasty. The capital was set in Yin-tien (Nanjing). He reigned from 1368 to 1399. The dynasty lasted 277 years (1368 - 1644) with 16 emperors.

TABLE 4. The Fokien Chapter II (continued)

Line-age	Parent/ Children	Dynasty/ (Emperor)	Year	Information
6	Tsung-yuan (2) --> Sar-lo (1st)	Ming/ (Tai-tzu) - (Chen-tzu)	1368 - 1413	Wife: Lee.
7	Sar-lo (1) --> Yu-ho	(Yin-tzong) - (Shi-tzong)	1462 - 1526	
8	Yu-ho (3) --> She-an (1st)	(Shen-tzong)- (Shi-tzong)	1484 - 1563	
9	She-an (3) --> Hsun-du (1st)	(Wu-tzong) - (?)	1514 - ?	
10	Hsun-du (2) --> Chun-chien (1st)	(Shi-tzong) - (?)	1540 - ?	
11	Chun-chien (5) --> How-hoh (5th)	(Shi-tzong) - (Zuan-leh)	1565 - 1633	

Nurhachu (1559-1629), a Manchu or a Nuechen and the emperor of the Posterior Jin, overthrew the Ming Dynasty. His son Huangtaichi changed the dynastic title to Ching. His grandson, the emperor Shun-tzu, was the first monarch of the Ching Dynasty (1644 - 1911). The dynasty lasted 268 years with 12 emperors, including Nurhachu and Huangtaichi.

| 12 | How-hoh (9) --> Sui-feng (3rd) | (Shun-tzong) - Ching/ (Kang-hsi) | 1608 - 1691 | |

TABLE 4. The Fokien Chapter II (continued)

Line-age	Parent/ Children	Dynasty/ (Emperor)	Year	Information
13	**Sui-feng (6)** --> *Guan-deh* --> *Guan-jiang* *(2nd)*	Ming/ (Zuan-leh) - Ching/ (Kang-hsi)	1642 - 1689	Guan-deh and Nan Kuan-neun, the daughter of a Commander in Chief. was an engaged couple, but he died young. His posthumous title "Dai-pae-kong," revealed that he was a man of high rank.
14	**Guan-jiang (7)** --> *Tien-tzung* *(1st)*	Ching/ (Kang-hsi) - (Yung-tseng)	1667 - 1729	Guan-jiang should be a man of high rank, too. After his elder brother had passed away, he was appointed to marry Nan Kuan-neun, who later dedicated a temple to her first fiancé. She lived **110** years, from 1667 to 1777.
15	**Tien-tzung (3)** -- > *Suii (1st)* - > *Tung* - > *Zuh*	(Kang-hsi) - (Cheng-long)	1695 - 1774	His wife Tong Liang lived from 1706 to 1778. The deaths of his second son, Tung, and third son Zuh, remain a riddle.

TABLE 5. The Taiwan Chapter

Line-age	Parent/Children	Dynasty/ (Emperor)	Year	Information
1 (16)	**Suii (3)** --> *Tsang (3rd)*	(Cheng-long)- (Jia-ching)	1736 - 1796	My great-great-great-grandfather came with his wife Nah Sham, 1739-1820, and three teenage sons from Fokien, China to Go-dun-leh, Taiwan in 1788.
2 (17)	**Tsang (4)** --> *Yi-zuh (3rd)*	(Cheng-long)- (Dau-kwang)	1776 - 1848	My great-great-grandmother Sun Hah, 1800 - 1876.
In 1895, Japan claimed Taiwan as her colony after the war Chia-Woo, the Sino-Japanese War of 1894.				
3 (18)	**Yi-zuh (4)** --> *Tsun-zwan* *(1st)*	(Dau-kwang)- Japanese (Mei-zii)	1831 - 1910	My great-grandfather was a scholarly farmer. My great-grandmother Liao Twen, 1834 - 1861.
4 (19)	**Tsun-zwan (4 sons and 7 daughters)** --> *Bun-hong (2nd)*	(Ceng-fong) - Japanese/ (Shiow-kga)	1856 - 1931	My grandfather, an intellectual, farming business-man, ran the village's only grocery store. My grandmother Tey Tsun, 1869 - 1939.
In 1945, Taiwan returned to the Republic of China after World War II.				

TABLE 5. The Taiwan Chapter (continued)

Line-age	Parent/Children	Dynasty/ (Emperor)	Year	Information
5 (20)	**Bun-fong (5 sons, 3 daughters)** -> *Deng-piao* -> *Deng-tzun* -> *Deng-kinm* -> *Deng-tzan* -> *Shiu-kim* -> *Shiu-bue* -> *Shiu-hu'ng* > *Deng-jiao*	Japanese/ (Mei-zii) - the Republic of China/ (President Chiang Kai-shek and President Chiang Jin-kou)	1898 - 1982	My father's life is shown at page 13. My mother Hsiao Pia lived only 52 years, 1898–1950. We always sigh in pain when remembering her short life as an ephemeral flower.

Deng-piao ran an import-export business for a time and retired after being a long-time land developer. He has written several unpublished books, using a Personal Computer as a writing tool when first at the age 72, and continues this pastime. Wife: Dune Sor-gyo (1925-1979). They have two daughters and one son.

Deng-tzun (1925-August 26, 1999) served more than 40 years as a Staff Civil Engineer at the Railroad Bureau. Saiyonana, Zi-hiang! When I eat *kgin-tze-kge* orange date preserves, I remember those old young days that you used to bring them home from Kgi-lan as a trip gift; today, I chew them with tears. When I hear the Japanese songs during the wartime, I remember those dark moonlit nights that you used to sing them in a thoughtful, melancholy mood; often, they echo in my heart. Wife: Kian Huei-ken. They have two sons and one daughter.

Deng-kinm ran his own architecture business and was a pioneer in this field in Taichung. He has just retired; he likes hiking and fishing. Wife: Ang Deh-hwa. They have two sons.

Deng-tzan retired from the largest government-owned civil engineering company in Taipei; he has been rehired as a consultant. See page 141 for his outstanding achievement. Wife: Dang Shor-tzeng. They have two daughters.

Shiu-kim worked many years as a mother to take care of us—younger siblings— and daily house chores, although she was only 16 years old, a high school girl, after my poor mother had passed away. She worked as an elementary school teacher before marrying. "Marry a chicken, follow a chicken; marry a dog, follow a dog," but she, a treetop phoenix, follows a dragon. Visiting a Chinese brush-painting class and playing golf, once a while, are her spare-time activities. Husband: Lau Zuh-yuh. They have two sons and one daughter.

TABLE 5. The Taiwan Chapter (continued)

Line-age	Parent/Children	Dynasty/ (Emperor)	Year	Information
				Shiu-bue had just graduated from the junior high school two months before our dear mother died. She stayed home in force and provided a pair of helping hands to Shiu-kim for this no-mother-hands' busy family. She continued her schools after our third sister-in-law Deh-hwa came to our family and provided us two mother-hands. Now, Shiu-bue has taught at an elementary school for more than 30 years. Having a passion for playing piano in her teens, she learned it through playing on her imaginative keyboard—drawing the black and white keys on a desk. Husband: Tzwa Tzun-hiung. They have two daughters and one son.
				Shiu-hu'ng is I. Julia is my Western name. There is a Chinese saying, "Living by a mountain, one makes a living relying on that mountain; living by a sea, one makes a living relying on that sea." I live in Silicon Valley, the largest computer industries center in the world, so I make a living relying on that computer industries — working on software engineering in the technical publication environment, although my original background is literature. Husband: Lim Dah-sheng. We have only one daughter.
				Deng-jiao retired in July of this year—1999—from the provincial Civil Engineering Department, where he served more than 25 years—many years as a section chief. Now, he starts his career's second Spring—running his own architecture business. Wife: Dang Quei-eng. They have three daughters.
				The three elder brothers started their careers early to help my father maintain the house budget of a family of ten.
				Deng-kinm, Deng-tzan, and Deng-jiao have passed the National High Civil Service Examination in the categories of architecture and civil engineering.

Swan
Song

"Hmm . . . , according to an old Chinese fairytale, she could be the moon, the fairy rabbit, which represents the year of 1999." This painting, two rabbits play under peonies, is created by my sister Shiu-kim to celebrate the year of Rabbit.

Swan Song

The joyful days of visiting Parasol Tree Village with my father are like a swiftly passing dream. To muse over memories of the past is bittersweet. While reflecting upon the dim and distant scenes, my eyes well over with tears. I have to learn that the dew-glistening morning glory is just another ephemeral flower, the neon-gleaming firefly is merely a fleeting insect, and a person living in the world is like a sojourner in an inn. What can I sigh other than "life is but a dream"?

While the song of life is transient as a spring dream, many poets, Western or Eastern, warn us: Don't waste your life wantonly! They say everyone is the life-smith of his or her own fortune; happiness is in your own golden hands. This acquired happiness is logical and convincing. However, the majority of Chinese believe that a person is born with a predetermined fate—success or failure—which was stamped at the time of birth—the year, month, day, and hour, which are the so-called Four Pillars of Life.

Happiness is out of one's control. The theory of this predestined happiness is self-denying and skeptical.

Interestingly, Chinese astrologers use the Four Pillars of Life to form a divination system called the Eight Characters Fate Interpretation. Each pillar is coded by using one stem of the Ten Celestial Stems (Chia, Yi, Ping, Ding, Wu, Chi, Geng, Hsin, Jen, Kuei) and one branch of the Twelve Terrestrial Branches (Tzi, Tzo, Yin, Mao, Tzun, Syh, Woo, Wei, Shen, Yeou, Hsu, Hai). So, there are eight characters for the four pillars. For example, the emperor Cheng-long had his Eight Characters[1] as "Hsin-Mao, Ding-Yeou, Geng-Woo, Ping-Tzi," which his grandfather the emperor Kang-hsi had interpreted as "Having an inherent life of wealth and honor" when the emperor Cheng-long was eleven years old.

The Ten Celestial Stems are further defined into a stem-branch system. "Stem" has strong cosmic elements and represents Yang (Wood: Fir, Fire: Burning wood, Earth: Hill, Metal: Weapons, Water: Waves) with odd numbers (**1.** Chia, **3.** Ping, **5.** Wu, **7.** Geng, **9.** Jen). "Branch" has weak cosmic elements and represents Yin (Wood: Bamboo, Fire: Lamp flame, Earth: Plain, Metal: Kettle, Water: Brooks) with even numbers (**2.** Yi, **4.** Ting, **6.** Chi, **8.** Hsin, **10.** Kuei). The dual combination (Chia-Yi, Ping-Ding, Wu-Chi, Geng-Hsin, Jen-Kuei) of each stem-branch, or Yang-Yin, or odd-even

---

1. It refers to *The Legend of the Emperor Cheng-long's Mao-Hare,* written by Du Lin on page F2 of *the World Journal* on February 16, 1999.

number has a close affinity to the planets (Wood star or Jupiter, Fire star or Mars, Earth star or Saturn, Metal star or Venus, Water star or Mercury). Each of the ten stems has an astrological name that stands for a certain stage of a tree's growth, to resemble the stages of life of a person.

The Twelve Terrestrial Branches represent a specific month of the year and are developed into a two-hour term of the day. Each branch has a corresponding animal. (**1.** Tzi=11-1 a.m. [Rat]; **2.** Tzo=1-3 [Ox]; **3.** Yin=3-5 [Tiger]; **4.** Mao=5-7 [Hare]; **5.** Tzun=7-9 [Dragon]; **6.** Syh=9-11 [Serpent]; **7.** Woo=11-1 p.m. [Horse]; **8.** Wei=1-3 [Sheep]; **9.** Shen=3-5 [Monkey]; **10.** Yeou=5-7 [Cock]; **11.** Hsu=7-9 [Dog]; and **12.** Hai=9-11 [Pig]). A full run of the twelve animals becomes a ring, which is thus twelve years.

A combination of the the Ten Celestial Stems and the Twelve Terrestrial Branches forms a sexagenary cycle. Chia-Tzi is the first combination of the cycle, so the sixty-year cycle is known as Chia-Tzi. The most recent Chia-Tzi cycle began in 1924 and ended in 1984.

The Eight Characters Fate Interpretation predicts a person's fate by interlocking the stem and the branch of each pillar with natural phenomena, including Five Cosmic Elements, Five Planets, Four Seasons (Spring, Summer, Autumn, Winter), and Five Directions (East, South, West, North, Center). Each of the matching rules or orders for expressing a pillar is rather complicated. To be able to explain it clearly, I would need to spend half my life to master it; hmm. . . , spending half a life for it would be too expensive and extravagant.

The popularity of the Eight Characters has not diminished in the least in these intellectual, civilized modern days. It is popular with engaged couples who check to see if both horoscopes harmonize or conflict. In the past, it used to be that the groom's family would ask the bride's family to provide her Eight Characters. Today, it is common for her side to ask also the time of his birth and to check whether his stars shine.

While many Chinese believe this divination system interprets a person's fate, whether flourishing or decaying, or merely use it as a reference for adjusting each stage of life, many other people are wise enough not to be trapped into this baseless labyrinth of popular belief.

Oh, no! That was a quick-tongued conclusion. It is not a maze; it is not baseless. Somehow, I do see the base with four pillars in it. It is arcane; it is mystic; it is obscure and unexplainable; and it is . . . . Hold my horses! I think I have to explain why I am seemingly not wise.

I was scared stiff and lost my tongue as I was reading my own Eight Characters Fate Interpretation. It is a tiny piece of red paper written by Lim Diau-pin Ceng (Remember? he was my father's sinology teacher) within the month after I was born. The predicted fate, written a half century ago, at certain points has mysteriously or coincidently somewhat agreed with my life.

The first time I saw this red paper was one night when I was a teenager and my father gathered all the red papers of his eight children and had fun reading each one. I remember he said that Deng-tzan, my fourth elder brother, would become an exceedingly talented dragon son, a fine offspring, and Shiu-kim, my eldest sister, would have a *fukuii-mian*, a life of opulence, like a peony. It turned out to be true and real, as true as real as gold. Deng-tzan received an award from President Lee Deng-huei for being the Most Outstanding Civil Engineer in 1997. Shiu-kim has married a prominent politician and has a wonderful life with two sons and a daughter. How uncanny that the prediction said in the red papers came true!

Three years ago, Deng-piao handed me a heavy envelope containing all my personal documents, including the tiny, red paper. This was the second time I had seen it, but I did not bother to open it until Sunday night, February 7, 1999—the night I concluded that the Eight Characters divination system was a baseless labyrinth—I had such an urge to read it on that moonlit night that it was as if someone had knocked at the door of my heart. Who was this obscure someone? Who was this messenger coming at this very moment to correct my prejudice? Hmm . . . , according to an old Chinese fairytale, she could be the moon, the fairy rabbit, which represents the year of 1999.

Lui Mong-tzeng, a premier and great scholar in the Sung Dynasty (960-1279), said that a person's fate is interwoven with luck to spell success. He said:

A man has great talent in a thousand ways; without luck,
the thoroughfare to success is obstructed.

The following epigram, which my uncle, using hair pencil, neatly wrote on classic rice paper, was mounted as an oversized wall scroll, which my father hung in our family dining room. In it, Lui Mong-tzeng sighed that success in life or happiness is dependent on time, luck, and fate, and these three elements are interwoven. We eight siblings had many fun times after dinner playing games by searching for words in this 560-word-long epigram.

Since many stanzas refer to historical events and the lives of their heroes, I skip them so you will not doze off while reading them. So, let me excerpt and translate two stanzas, in which he counseled further that fate is immutable, interwoven not only with luck but also with time.

A centipede has a hundred feet,
>   but it crawls no faster than a snake.

A turtledove has two wings,
>   but it flies no higher than a raven.

A horse runs a thousand miles;
>   without a rider, it runs not far.

A person has sky-reaching ambition;
>   without luck, the sky is not reachable.

If the heaven is not in its time,
>   the sun and moon do not shine.

If the earth is not in its time,
>   ten thousand things do not grow.

If the water is not in its time,
>   the waves do not surge.

If a person is not in his (her) time,
>   luck does not come.

If fate were not predetermined by the stem-branched
>   Eight Characters, who would not wish to be wealthy
>   and high-standing rather than resignedly to be
>   destitute and low-standing?

T his epigram reflects upon the fate of the swans in this book. Now, before ending my song and cleaning my bamboo flute, let all those luckless, or born-at-the-wrong-time swans utter their own bitter-sweet songs.

1. Lim-Hsiao Pia, an ephemeral flower: "Luck—having eight children but with no days to see them all grow up—for me was like flowers in a mirror and the moon on the water; it was solely appealing but not real. Wipe your tears away and don't cry for my short life, my dears!"

2. Lim Bun-hong, a mute victim of the changing of the system of government: "Diligence and Frugality are golden and the parents of good luck. With this rule I survived the non-Beijing tongue and that awful currency depreciation—exchanging OT$ 40,000.00 for NT$ 1.00."[2]

3. The grand old tree at the brook-head, the sashed Kgar-dong tree: "I wish I had grown up at the brook-end so that the absentminded emperor's messenger would not have mixed up me with my young fellow brother."

4. Lim Tung and Lim Zuh, two immortal peach eaters who ascended to the Peach Blossom utopia: "What a joke we played on you—writing our story on water, so that no one can solve the riddle of our death."

---

2. This exploitation policy was annonced on June 15, 1949. The rate was not worth exchanging since the bills could be used as bathroom tissues for 40, 000 times. O(N)T$ = Old (New) Taiwan Dollar.

---

5. Pi Kan, the progenitor of Lim: "Dah-chi would envy me today, knowing that my family tree has burgeoned worldwide and that my family line is now in its 105th generation or higher, having 3,133 rings so far."

6. Lim Quan-hu'ng, the elected imperial court marshal: "I was told to reach the sun, but I got burned by it. The truth is that health outweighs fame and fortune."

7. Lim Keng-sheng, the well-learned scholar: "As Yin rose over Yang, the sky was changed and I was like an overlaid bamboo shoot that never had a chance to break through the soil."

8. Lim Sung-bun, the unsung hero: "I miscalculated the emperor Cheng-long's stellar light, which was really brighter than mine; too bad, I should have checked it with an astrologer beforehand."

9. Lim Mo-neun, Ma-tzo-po, the Goddess of All Trades: "It was heaven's decree to die young, but my worshippers have spoiled me—the smoke curls up constantly from the incensories, and the flowers perpetually perfume the altars."

Look up! It is spring again. It is the time that a file of swans, flying in pairs and wing to wing, are high in the sky. Where are they flocking to? Where? Ah! Of course, they are going to their home village—Parasol Tree Village.